D0926675

Understanding
The MALE EGO

Understanding
The MALE EGO

Peter & Evelyn Blitchington

THOMAS NELSON PUBLISHERS
Nashville • Camden • New York

Published in Nashville, Tennessee, by Thomas Nelson, Inc., and distributed in Canada by Lawson Falle, Ltd., Cambridge, Ontario.

Printed in the United States of America.

Unless otherwise noted all Scripture quotations are from the NEW KING JAMES VERSION. Copyright © 1979, 1980, 1982, Thomas Nelson, Inc., Publishers.

Scripture quotations marked TLB are from *The Living Bible* (Wheaton, Illinois: Tyndale House Publishers, 1971) and are used by permission.

Scripture quotations marked NIV are from the Holy Bible: New International Version. Copyright © 1978 by the New York International Bible Society. Used by permission of Zondervan Bible Publishers.

Scripture quotations marked KJV are from the King James Version of the Bible.

Scripture quotations marked MOFFAT are from *The Bible: A New Translation by James Moffat*, Copyright 1950. Published by Harper and Brothers.

Library of Congress Cataloging in Publication Data

Blitchington, Peter.
  Understanding the male ego.

  Includes bibliographical references.
  1. Men—Psychology. 2. Ego (Psychology) 3. Sex role.
I. Blitchington, Evelyn, 1947-   . II. Title.
HQ1090.B55   1984   155.6′32   84-2154
ISBN 0-8407-5327-6

Contents

Understanding
The MALE EGO

ONE

This Book's For You!

While reading the newspaper several days ago, I came across an article about Robert, a man who had chosen to stand on the sidelines during the battles over women's rights. He didn't campaign vigorously for the ERA, but neither did he oppose his wife's interest in feminism. He tried to remain neutral, doing his "fair share" both at home and at work.

But Robert felt lonely and isolated. Everyone was focusing on the needs and rights of women. Every time he opened a magazine or watched the evening news, it seemed he was being given some new bit of information on womanhood.

"What about men?" he asked himself. "Why doesn't someone talk about their needs, their role in a changing society? Men have problems and needs that women just don't understand."

So Robert formed a men's support group to address the plight of men who are caught in the middle of a changing society. He put up posters; he talked with people; he placed ads in the newspaper. And he found that, just as he suspected, many men were experiencing what he was—loneliness and isolation.

Frequently men told how they felt under attack, but weren't exactly sure what part of themselves was threatened. They sensed that they should defend something, but didn't know what to defend or even if the defense would be worth the effort.

Women sense this confusion among men, too. As a twenty-six-year-old female writer for a large newspaper noted, "Men have never been so narcissistic—or so perplexed—about what they are."

In this book, we will discuss the cornerstone of masculine nature—the male ego. We will look at the many aspects of manhood with the purpose of enabling the reader—whether male or female—to grasp what it means to be a man in today's changing world.

The title of the book contains the word *understanding.* We chose this word because we want the reader to have an increased awareness and appreciation of factors that make up the male ego.

We decided that to promote real understanding, we needed to write a book that would be relevant for both men and women. We wanted to include material that would help women understand the male ego and enable them to deal effectively with ego problems in their own men. So the first half of the book is written with women in mind.

Some of the descriptions we offer will apply to "men in general," that is, factors that mold the egos or are expressions of the egos of a large proportion of the population. The chapter entitled, "Why Won't My Husband Help Me Around the House?" for example, takes a look at the typical pattern for division of household labor in most homes. It attempts to explain via a description of male ego development why men usually aren't more actively involved in home duties.

Other chapters look at such topics as how the male ego is wrapped up in sex and how men think more in terms of laws and principles while women are more concerned with relationships (along with a discussion of what this has to do with male and female ego development).

We also wanted a book that would help men acquire greater ego strength. So the second half is directed toward them.

The central task for the healthy person is to acquire a positive sense of self-worth. That is, in our opinion, the central part of sound emotional development for all people. In addition to that, for every man the pivotal component of a healthy ego is a sound sense of *masculine* self-worth.

Chapter nine, for example, is designed to help men acquire a healthy definition of their own masculine self-worth. The definition of self-worth that we choose to adopt will automatically engender a set of beliefs and interpretations about the world. Those beliefs and interpretations help determine a man's emotional adjustment to the world and his response to good and bad events that occur in his life. Those beliefs and interpretations are discussed in chapter ten.

Finally, the last chapter is entitled "The Higher Purpose." It sums up the most important experiences that affect the male ego and offers a framework for providing men with a sense of purpose beyond themselves, which can serve as an ennobling and elevating influence upon their egos.

As important as it is to provide an intellectual understanding of men and their egos, we have not made this our sole aim. Information alone, no matter how insightful, will be of little benefit unless the reader uses this information to improve his or her life.

We realize that we must not only provide basic concepts and facts but that we must also apply them to practical areas of living. Thus we have given some very specific suggestions on how women can handle men with ego problems and how men can rethink or reevaluate their own experiences. We have tried to give alternative suggestions, too, because we realize that one idea won't work for all people.

How We Wrote the Book

The process of putting this book together sometimes led to ego conflicts. Both of us have written books alone, but this was our first joint effort. We decided that the book would be written in Peter's voice, since that seemed to make the anecdotes easier to read. So the "I's" refer to Peter.

Our first decision was how to divide up the writing. We quickly abandoned the process of writing together, since that caused us to bump our heads together constantly. But after experimenting, we found that our differences were actually blessings in disguise. I think in terms of ideas, facts, and research; Evelyn focuses on anecdotes and illustrations, making the ideas practical. So I was responsible for the basic structure and content of the book. I wrote out the ideas for all the chapters, and Evelyn went back over the material and fleshed it out with anecdotes and other illustrations. Because we recognized, admitted, and accepted our differences, we were able to produce a better book together than either of us could have done alone.

Our experiences in learning to write together illustrate our ultimate aim for this book: to promote understanding and acceptance of the male ago in all facets, and to provide practical ways for men and women to work together to reconcile and capitalize on their differences. We seek to make your life better with a man or as a man.

But before we launch into our discussion of the male experience, we will take a few pages to answer the question, "Just what is an ego, anyway?"

Part 1

FOR WOMEN WHO WANT TO UNDERSTAND THEIR MEN

TWO

What Is An Ego?

Janice constantly finds herself at odds with her husband over the way he handles his sexual drive. "Bill usually comes home from work angry and frustrated. The people at work are on his back all day long, but he waits until he comes home and then takes it out on me. He criticizes nearly everything I do. To make matters worse, just about the time I'm totally discouraged and devastated by his negative attitude, he'll want to make love! If I go along with him, I feel used, but I don't want to make a scene, either. He has so many pressures at work, and I don't want to add one more."

Robert lost his job about eight months ago. After the initial shock and hurt wore off, he waged an aggressive campaign to find work. He went to employment agencies, read newspaper want ads, went on every interview he could get, and sent job resumés all over town. But when no job was forthcoming, he became more and more listless, spending much of his time on the sofa watching TV. He wouldn't help his wife around the house, even though she had a full-time job. He even refused to chauffeur the kids around to their afternoon activities. Now it looks like his marriage may be breaking up, too.

At their high school reunion, several men enjoyed a hearty laugh as they remembered the antics of a classmate named Frank.

"Remember how Frank had to win at everything? Tennis, badminton, Monopoly, track, . . . it didn't matter what he played as long as he could come out on top."

What Is An Ego?

"Boy, do I remember! Once I was playing chess with him, and it looked like I was about to win. He got really nervous; his leg started bouncing up and down, and he shifted back and forth in his seat. Right before I won, he 'accidentally' knocked over the board, and we just quit playing. He kept saying that he hadn't done it on purpose, but I knew better. I noticed, too, that he never wanted to play chess with me after that."

Tension is mounting at Terry's house. He knows that he deserves a raise; his wife knows it, too—she tells him often enough.

"Terry, why don't you just go into your supervisor's office tomorrow morning and ask for more money? With all the overtime you put in, you certainly have earned it." But Terry just won't ask. His wife feels totally frustrated by his lack of initiative; it reminds her too much of when she and Terry were dating.

"I've been through this before," she remembers. "Terry and I had dated for two years; we were deeply in love; our educations were behind us. But he never did ask me to marry him. We both knew that we were going to get married one day, but he just couldn't (or wouldn't) pop the question. So I had to."

Lisa doesn't know whether to laugh or cry. Her boyfriend Burt has some comment to make about everything she does: "Lisa, your hair is too short." "Lisa, you act too nervous around my parents. You need to learn to relax." "Lisa, you're so slow. Why does it take you an hour and a half to get ready to go to the beach?"

Lisa really loves Burt, but she finds all of this "advice" a little hard to take. She wishes he would just let her be herself. The funny thing about Burt, though, is that while he has all sorts of criticism to give Lisa, she can't even offer a single suggestion to him. If she says anything at all negative to him, he wilts on the spot and doesn't get over it for days.

When we decided to write a book on the male ego, we began our research by finding out what the term "male ego" meant to other people. We conducted a variety of interviews and came up with dozens of stories like the ones we've outlined above. Though we never intended these interviews to constitute a scientific sample, we couldn't help but make some generalizations from them. We learned, for example, that people have strong feelings about the male ego. However difficult it seems to be to clearly define an ego, men and women respond to the term immediately and with clear understanding. Most people can come up with a perceptive response right off the top of their heads. Apparently they give much thought to this topic.

Unfortunately, we seem to be able to understand what an ego is better than we are able to define it. Even though every person we talked to immediately understood our questions about the "male ego," when we asked for a definition of the term, much disagreement resulted.

Professionals in the field of human behavior also find the concept difficult to define. Psychologists writing in the professional literature, for example, define the term *ego* differently from non-psychologists.

Our own definition of ego corresponds more closely with those we heard among lay people than with those we found among psychologists. *We see "ego" as a very broad attribute comprising a variety of experiences, traits, and attitudes.* We offer the following diagram to represent the structure of the ego:

At the very core of the ego lies the sense of *self-worth*. Here the question, "How important am I as a person?" is answered rationally. This is a relatively stable trait, not fluctuating a great deal up or down depending upon circumstances or mood swings. This very important component strongly influences all the remaining parts of the

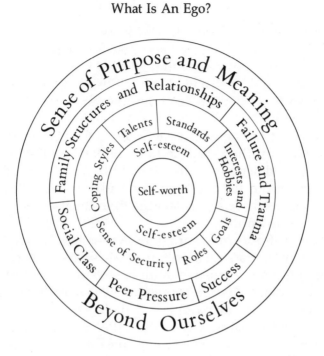

ego; it in turn is influenced by the other ego components.

Self-esteem is the next most important attribute. It is more of an emotional attribute of self-value, while self-worth is more of an intellectual assessment. Generally, when the sense of self-worth is strong, self-esteem will also be high. But it is possible for self-esteem to be low while self-worth is strong. (The reverse is not true.)

A friend of ours recently went through a painful divorce in which his ex-wife assaulted him emotionally on every possible front. She questioned his morals, his sense of responsibility to his children, his business ethics, and even his virility. This dealt a crushing blow to his self-esteem; but after the shock wore off, his sense of self-worth remained intact. He knew his life had importance, even if he was on the downside right then. He knew he could make a worthwhile contribution to mankind, so he gritted his teeth and began to rebuild his shattered life.

Everyone has periods in life when their self-esteem is very low, but they are able to go on because they still have a solid sense of self-worth. In fact, we've known people who are not overburdened with high self-esteem and yet they have a persistent faith in themselves; that faith is self-worth.

After self-esteem, a variety of experiences, generally equal in importance, contribute to ego strength. A basic *sense of security,* a trusting attitude toward life and people, is molded first and foremost by our early family experiences. If our parents did their jobs reasonably well, we have that basic security. If they didn't, our lives are colored by a vague sense of uneasiness and pessimism about the world and the people who make it up.

The skills we've inherited and acquired that enable us to cope with events and people play a strong role in our ego development. Those *coping skills* evolve from our temperaments, talents, and early family background. Closely related to coping skills, the *roles* we've learned to fill, our success at performing them, and how much respect they are generally given influence the structure of our egos.

Our *talents* contribute to our ego development, as do our *interests*. These attributes give us direction for our energies and an outlet for our creativity. The view our society has of those talents and interests influences our self-esteem. If we are very adept at memorization and can rattle off the names, birthdates, and years in office of every president from George Washington to Ronald Reagan, this talent won't do our egos much good if no one in society values this skill.

Finally, at this third level of ego structure, our *goals* and *standards* guide us and give criteria for comparing the ideal self (the person we'd like to be) with the real self (the person we actually are).

At the fourth level of ego structure we find those experiences that have molded us as we developed and continue to influence our egos today, albeit to a smaller degree than the ones covered already.

Our early *family structure and relationships* play the strongest role in our ego development. The relationship we have with our parents, along with our birth order position in the family, govern the way our egos unfold. For men, the childhood relationship with the father is especially important, for the father either helps or impedes his son's acquisition of a secure sense of masculinity.

The *social class* we come from molds the way we act and think. Sociological studies have shown that people from the middle and upper social classes feel more in control of their lives, have a greater sense of autonomy, and are more optimistic about the future than those from the lower social classes. Of course, money and occupational prestige play a role. But people from the higher social classes generally direct and manage others while people from the lower social classes are directed and managed by others. Finally, social class is a mild predictor of husband-wife relationships. In the upper social classes, husbands and wives are more equalitarian than they are in the lower social classes.

Our histories of *successes,* on one hand, and *failures and traumas,* on the other, influence our sense of ego security. Those of us who have enjoyed a history of satisfying successes with intermittent failures usually have stronger egos than those who have experienced mainly failures with intermittent successes. However, failure creates a certain discipline and determination in many people, and how a person deals with success and failure depends on all the ego components we've discussed so far. Overly easy and quick successes often lead to a weaker, rather than a stronger, ego. (Consider Elvis Presley and Freddie Prinze, for example.)

Finally, at the fourth level, our history of *peer group relationships* molds the way we think about ourselves and the structure of our egos. A pecking order always unfolds among children and adolescents, with those at the top acquiring different ego experiences from those at the bottom. Physical attractiveness, athletic and social skills, and personality traits such as dominance help determine our position in the hierarchies. And our hierarchical positions help determine the way we relate to other people.

These experiences and traits determine the extent to which a person achieves the fifth level—*a sense of purpose and meaning beyond the self.* When we have a sense of self-worth and a healthy self-esteem, and when we have had enough of the positive experiences at the intermediate levels, we can turn our attention outward, toward something higher than ourselves. But if we lack some crucial experience at one of the earlier levels, our attention is diverted away from a high purpose and toward attempts to compensate for the deficit. This diversion accounts for what we usually call "ego problems."

Of course, real-life experiences are more dynamic than our diagram suggests. Many of our traits and experiences do not produce permanent attributes; they are subject to changes that require reorganization of the entire diagram. Our self-esteem goes up or down, our family changes, we move up in social class, we have a series of successes or failures, and so on. Those experiences create changes to which we must adjust. But if the core is solid, we will have a stronger ego and be more successful in adapting to changing circumstances.

THREE

Why Won't My Husband Help Me Around the House?

Recently my wife and I had two couples over for dinner. Together, our two sets of guests provided a range of lifestyles. One couple had two children, and the wife stayed home to take care of them. The other couple were childless, career-oriented people with master's degrees in business administration.

As we talked, strong differences in values and goals revealed themselves, especially between the women. They disagreed about such topics as the role of women, the desirability of having children, and the ideal pattern for marriage. But when the topic shifted to the male ego, and particularly to the way men conduct themselves around the home, these women began to speak a common language.

Harry, a twenty-seven-year-old with a new MBA and an even newer job as a "systems engineer," served as the catalyst.

"What exactly does a systems engineer do?" asked Linda, the mother of the two children.

"I'm involved with food management," Harry answered. "We look for ways to improve the handling and delivery of perishable materials, such as food, in hospitals."

"How do you do that?" someone else asked.

Harry, warming to the task, began to explain his job further: "We store the food in ice bins; then we take it to the central processing unit where it's rethermalized."

Linda, looking confused, asked, "What do these terms mean—'central processing unit' and 'rethermalizing'?"

Before Harry could answer, his wife, Marilyn, chimed in: "All it means is that they freeze the food, put it in refrigerators, ship it to the kitchen, and cook it. The central processing unit is the kitchen and rethermalizing just means to cook it."

"Why don't they just use ordinary terms, like 'kitchen' and 'cooking'?" Linda asked Harry.

Again Marilyn interrupted, with a sly smile on her face: "Because this service is run by men, and if they called it kitchen and cooking, the job would be too demeaning, and they'd lose interest in it."

Is this also what goes on between men and women in the home? Do men resist equal sharing of household roles because they see housework as demeaning?

I suspect the answer is more complicated than that. But somehow the male ego seems to demand a division of labor in order to feel secure.

In fact, studies indicate that fathers are much more involved in differentiating the roles and personalities of their sons and daughters than are mothers. And men seem compelled to avoid jobs that have come to be known as "woman's work," no matter how rewarding they are in reality. For example, traditionally we have thought of medicine as a masculine field because most physicians in the United States are male. But in the Soviet Union, over 75 percent of physicians are women. After Soviet medicine became known as a feminine field, many men began to avoid it like the plague. They took their energy into physics, and jobs associated with the space race suddenly became a field in which men could affirm their masculinity. They left medicine to women and to less threatened men.

So, many men do seem to need a separation between masculine and feminine in order to feel secure. (Have you noticed, for example, anything unique about male airline stewards? Every one I've seen has at least a mustache, and often a beard also.) And the need is even more apparent in the home.

The facts are consistent. The average woman spends approximately fifty-three hours a week doing household tasks (cleaning, cooking, grocery shopping, transporting children) while the average man spends only a few hours a week at those tasks, whether his wife works full time or not.[1]

Apparently the lack of devotion to household chores is not only characteristic of American men. Eastern and western European, Soviet, Scandinavian, and Oriental men show approximately the same pattern.

The explanation that men consider housework, or other "women's work," too demeaning doesn't seem to tell the entire story. For one thing, the most "demeaning" jobs (e.g., garbage collecting) are held by men, not women. Further, jobs around the home that are considered "masculine," such as cutting the grass or taking out the garbage, are no more inherently attractive or uplifting than the "feminine" jobs.

Something more powerful than the desire to avoid "demeaning" tasks seems to be at work here. Men and women march to the beat of music that is extremely resistant to tampering or modification.

For example, Barbara Forisha, a psychologist at the University of Michigan, wrote an elaborate book in which she reviewed the research on sex roles in the home among young, modernistic couples.[2] Most of these couples had started marriage with the firm intention of establishing completely equalitarian labor divisions. There would be no division of labor into the traditional pattern. Husbands and wives were committed to an equalitarian goal.

But despite their best intentions, the marriage arrangement soon began to drift toward the traditional pattern. Dr. Forisha concluded,

Couples who share the management of finances and household responsibilities in their first years of marriage slowly slip into traditional sex-typed divisions of labor after five years of marriage. Joint decision-making policies often become male-dominated policies, and married women begin to define their husband's role as the "breadwinner" and their own role as the "mother and homemaker."

This drift into the traditional pattern was not thrust upon the wives by their husbands. Both partners collaborated in the shift. In fact, in those homes where couples started out by dividing responsibilities equally in a nontraditional fashion, *the wives were often the first partners who became dissatisfied with that arrangement and began to resist their husband's efforts to take over responsibilities in the kitchen and the home.* Apparently, powerful forces are at work here to compel couples to adopt the traditional pattern.

One likely contributor to the sexual division of labor is biology. Research does indicate that males and females are "wired" differently in the central nervous system.

[27]

Psychologists Anne Erhardt and Susan Baker found that females who had been exposed to male hormones during that critical time in the womb when their brains were rapidly developing ended up with masculine personality traits such as aggressiveness and initiative.[3] Other studies, with both animals and humans, have verified these findings. Men and women are biologically different in a way that influences their personality traits.

These findings no doubt provide some of the reasons why men and women drift into a sexual division of labor in the home. Also, many men associate being taken care of in the home with being loved. But something even more fundamental seems to be at work here. Male energy seems to be channeled in such a way that men feel impelled to separate their activities from those of women. Their very identities as men are dependent upon their carving out a role that is separate from that of their wives.

Men in Search of a Role

I had been counseling for only four months when Dick Morrison, my first terminally ill client, walked in. I must admit that I faced the interview with some anxiety; what exactly do you say to someone who knows he's dying?

Dick had worked in the coal mines most of his life and had contracted a fatal lung disease. When I first met him, he had only a few years to live. During the hour-long interview, Dick and I discussed many issues: his fears of dying, his children by a previous marriage, the pain of his lung disease, the loss of his physical powers, and all the things he had never done and never would do. But the topic that dominated the conversation was his inability to provide for the woman he loved and what that meant for the two of them—no marriage.

"I'm not a man anymore. When Sue and I first met, we talked a lot about getting married. But now that's out of the question. I'm totally disabled; there's no way I can provide for her. I really want to work and make a good living for Sue. But I can't."

Dick's inability to provide seemed to cripple his very identity and security as a man.

Somehow, at the core of man's ego lies the need to provide, the need to support his wife and family. This is the most tangible role linking a man to his family. The wife may be the queen of the home, the object of the children's devotion and dependence; but the husband provides the castle for them to live in; he makes possible the lifestyle that they enjoy; he carries the major responsibility for supplying necessities and luxuries for his wife and children.

Recently several women have come in to me for counseling with the same problem: their husbands are out of work, making the wives the sole providers. But that's not their main complaint. The problem is the way their husbands act after they lose their jobs.

"He won't do anything productive around the home now that he's out of work," complained one woman. "He actually does less housework now than he did when he had a job. I have it all on my back—all the work. And I get no support from him."

Another woman—married, thirty years old, with two young children—described an even darker, but surprisingly common, result of unemployment. "He gets mad and hits the children," she said as tears welled up in her eyes, "and he's beaten me up, too. He's always sorry afterward," she added quickly, "but he doesn't seem to get any better."

Men are usually devastated by the loss of their jobs, much to the chagrin and dismay of their wives. Their work is more than simply a paycheck or a way to structure their time. It is their door to the family—to a wife and children. Without the role of provider, a man simply cannot compete with a woman. She has too powerful an advantage: she is much more confident in and comfortable about her identity than he is about his.

A woman carries her role in her own body. She is elegantly designed to bear children and nurture them through breastfeeding. It is physically impossible for a man to fulfill her role, and so she never has to face the question, "Am I really important for the survival of the family?" She has tangible evidence of her own importance. She may be hurt and discouraged if she loses a job. But she doesn't experience that desperation born of a threat to her most basic sense of self.

Consider a man's plight, however. His body dictates only one role: sexual release. Aside from this, every other role he assumes must be assigned to him by society. As Margaret Mead observed, "The central problem of every society is to define appropriate roles for the men."[4] In other words, a man relies more on external roles for a sense of security than does a woman. For his ego to remain strong, society's role for him must be as ennobling as possible, giving him a firm link to the family, helping him feel that he makes an important and necessary contribution.

One role has been consistently set aside for men—providing for the family. In societies where men hunt for food, their egos tend to be strongest, possibly because hunting is an activity seldom engaged in by women.[5] The male hunters know that their families depend heavily upon them for food; they feel needed and important. Male egos are somewhat weaker in agricultural society, depending upon how much the women are involved in gardening. If women not only care for the home and children, but also help with the gardening, a man may feel that he is dispensable, that life could go along pretty well without him.

Thus, society defines the man's role, and that role in turn influences his ego strength. But male insecurity is even more pervasive than that. The restless energy that most men display is tied to a basic insecurity. Men must perform in order to feel like men. But their performance has a purpose.

Why Can't He Just Relax?

Recently I felt the need for a break from work, so I took the day off, and my wife and I took the children to Circus World. Since we went in the middle of the week, and the weather was quite cool, Circus World was almost deserted. We could walk right up to any attraction without a wait, so we were able to do much more than usual. We discovered that when a few people had a whole amusement park to themselves, there were two attractions that consistently kept the people coming back. The roller coaster stood idle for most of the day, as did the centrifugal-force ride. But the people lined up for the bumper cars and the test of strength.

At the bumper cars, children, teen-agers, and adults delighted in crashing into each other and swerving to avoid someone crashing into them. There were endless head-on collisions and rear-end smash-ups. When the ride ended, you could hear a collective sigh, followed immediately by a mass stampede toward the exit, as everyone raced to get back in line and do it again. Since the crowds were sparse, many people rode the cars twenty or thirty times in a row, never seeming to tire of it.

Close by the bumper cars stood the test of strength attraction, where an individual hit a block with a sledge hammer and a ball would fly up a pole to indicate how much pressure he'd managed to apply. On the pole were numbers from zero to one hundred. When some lucky person hit the block just right and very hard, sending the ball all the way up to one hundred, a siren would go off, alerting everyone for hundreds of yards around of his accomplishment.

Our family walked by this attraction early in the day and saw several men trying unsuccessfully to hit the top. In fact, no one made the ball rise higher than seventy. The man running this attraction consoled each one with the fact that, "No one makes it on the first try. You have to work on your technique." So the contestants kept handing over fifty cents for three tries at the hundred mark. One man especially stood out—he had to use two canes to walk up to the block and then had to support himself with the canes while he swung the sledge hammer. He was very persistent, returning to the block at least three times during the few minutes we watched. Between tries he returned to a wheelchair.

Our family walked on, took in the main circus performance, let the children go on each of their rides once more, and then returned to the bumper cars and the test of strength one last time. The "old faithful" ones were still crashing their cars into each other at the bumper car ride, but now the sound of smashing cars was interspersed every few minutes by the sound of the siren from the test of strength.

We wandered over to see what was happening and saw, to our surprise, the same group of men who had been there earlier in the day. The man with the canes was still trying unsuccessfully to hit the hundred mark, but a friend of his had discovered "the technique." By the time we got there he had won four bears in Swiss outfits and was about to win another. Between turns, he encouraged his friends to keep on trying and described in detail the method that was working so successfully for him. Although he eventually depleted the operator's stockpile of prizes and brought out several Circus World officials to see what was going on, he kept on playing . . . and winning. I overheard him tell his friends as he left the park with five bears and three frogs, "It's nice to know that there's at least one thing I can do well."

Many men, it seems, display that need to perform, that need to excel, that relentless drive to prove themselves in some area. You see it in little boys as they tell their friends, "I can run faster than you can," in early teens as they ride their bicycles, not in the normal way but with no hands or only on the back tire, in young men as they cruise around in their "souped-up" cars, and in adult men as they strive for success, prestige, money, or power. Mediocrity isn't what they're seeking. An average job, a regular car, a passive acceptance of life—those things hold little appeal for many men.

The restless desire for activity and performance has not gone unnoticed by students of human behavior.

Medical researchers have classified all people into two groups according to "coronary proneness." One group they call Type A, the other Type B. Type A individuals seem to be involved in an ongoing struggle to master their environment, to obtain as many "things" as possible, in the very shortest time period, whether those things be material possessions, achievements, or even ideas. Type A people are driven. Type B individuals, on the other hand, are relaxed, content, unhurried. Not surprisingly, Type A individuals are more likely to develop several kinds of heart disease than are Type Bs.

Recently I read the transcript of a seminar given by a noted cardiac specialist. As a young man he had been keenly competitive, working long, hard hours to establish himself as an expert in his field of medicine. There just weren't enough hours in the day for him to accomplish all he wanted to do. But early in life he was struck down with heart disease and had to abandon his former career. He now goes all over the country giving stress-management seminars in an effort to help other people avoid the mixture of excessive competitiveness and unbridled desire for "everything right now" that almost cost him his life.

In his seminar, that physician made a statement that really caught my eye. He has studied Type A and Type B individuals quite extensively, and he has found that 80 percent of men fall into the Type A classification. Only about one man in five feels satisfied with his life; only one in five sees no real urgency to change the status quo.

What keeps 80 percent of men from relaxing and appreciating what they have? What drives them on and on? The usual explanation is that society has conditioned men that way. Little girls are taught that it's un-ladylike to be assertive; little boys learn that they have to go after what they want, letting nothing get in their way. Or so the theory goes. Even fairy tales picture young women waiting for their knights in shining armor to arrive; the men, meanwhile, gain nothing by waiting, but must hammer out their own armor and go run down the horse to ride on.

But conditioning by society cannot fully explain why the majority of men find themselves in an endless search for accomplishment and activity. A man's urge to perform and prove himself has its basis in real processes, some of which begin early in life.

George Gilder, in *Sexual Suicide*,[6] describes the struggle a male goes through to establish his sexual identity. As an infant he finds comfort, security, and sustenance in the arms of his mother. But during the early stages of toddlerhood, he discovers that he is indeed quite different from his mother; he is growing up to be a daddy, not a mommy. He cannot wear Mom's clothes, Mom's cologne, or Mom's make-up as his sister can. He can, however, wear Dad's after-shave lotion, Dad's hat, and shave with Dad's razor.

The young boy is caught in a no-man's land. He cannot be like his mom, with whom he has such close emotional ties; he must be like his dad, who is nearly always more distant and unavailable, if only because he is gone from home so much. Still, the boy longs for a close tie with a woman, and in adult life he is granted that privilege by asserting "his manhood in action." Unlike a girl, who enters womanhood at the beginning of menstruation, a boy has no one conclusive biological signal for the beginning of manhood, so society has to set up some "rite of passage" to announce his entrance into adulthood. These rites of passage can vary anywhere from killing a lion (among the Zulu) to finding a job (in America). But a boy must prove himself worthy of being called a man; he must perform some action in order to enter adulthood.

And a man's search for sexual identity doesn't stop after he successfully completes his rite of passage. Being a man is a fragile state, which can be lost. Unless a man constantly affirms his masculinity, he feels unsure of his own sexual identity.

This concept seems almost foreign to women, who have little or no trouble believing that they are truly female. Rarely do you hear, "I just don't feel like a woman anymore." It usually takes a very traumatic experience, such as a mastectomy or hysterectomy, to make a woman feel insecure about her sexual identity.

Men, on the other hand, face loss of their feeling of masculinity in many subtle ways. Almost anything that reduces his ability to have an impact on the world can threaten a man's sexual identity. Retirement, illness, failure, a crippling accident—all of these circumstances, as varied and uncontrollable as they are, can endanger a man's ego, causing him either to give up on himself or redouble his efforts to prove his masculinity.

Jake had a serious case of diabetes, which left him unable to walk more than a few yards and destroyed all feeling in his feet. Much to Jake's annoyance, his son had to drive him to the doctor's office for his monthly appointments. He wanted so much to at least be able to drive himself to the doctor. It was bad enough to be crippled, but to be crippled and dependent on his son was too much for him to bear.

One day Jake got ready for his doctor's appointment,

just as usual, and hobbled out to the car to wait for his son to arrive. But when his son was a few minutes late, Jake took the situation into his own hands. He slipped over into the driver's seat, cranked up the car, and headed down the road toward town. By the time he got to the doctor's office, he was so weak that two nurses had to help him into the building. But even though he received a lecture from his doctor, got the whole family thoroughly upset, and needed a vitamin B-12 shot just to have the energy to drive back home, Jake felt that he had achieved a victory. He had proved to himself and others that he could still take care of himself. He arrived home with renewed ego strength, with a stronger sense of his own masculinity.

Glenn reacted to an ego-threatening situation in a very different manner. He had a successful dry-cleaning business, a nice home, and a wife and children who loved him dearly. But when the recession brought massive unemployment to his hometown, Glenn's business dropped to less than half its usual rate. Glenn heard about an opening at a large cleaning plant about one hundred miles away; he went for an interview and accepted the job on the spot. He sold his business and his home and moved his family. But things went poorly on the new job almost from the first. Glenn's employer was dishonest and thoughtless in his dealings with his employees. Glenn's wife pushed him to stand up for his rights; but Glenn, having already experienced what he considered failure in his own business, decided to keep quiet and just take the abusive treatment. Eventually things got so bad that Glenn quit his job and moved his family back home where he took a job paying minimum wages.

Glenn's ego first came under attack when he lost his

business; but rather than fighting to reestablish his self-esteem as did Jake, he became psychologically castrated. He began to feel that he was no longer a man, especially after the second job fell through. He surrendered to self-doubt. Rather than trying to prove himself again, rather than putting his ego on the line one more time, he took a low-paying job and decided to be content with what he had.

The experiences of both Jake and Glenn point out how insecure men feel about their own masculinity, how quickly they can lose their identity. This male insecurity translates either into a striving for performance, a quest for the reaffirmation of male sexual identity, or a retreat from performance, a withdrawal from the rat race of trying to prove manhood.

Women may feel amused or even a little irritated as they watch men constantly having to prove themselves. "James has a good job with plenty of prestige, a generous salary, and enough time off. Why can't he be satisfied? Lots of men would give their right arm to be in his shoes."

Given these male ego problems—the need for a special role in the home and a basic sexual insecurity—it's not hard to see why a sexual division of labor solidifies in every culture and in practically every home.

FOUR

Different Types of Men, Different Egos

In previous chapters, we've looked at some general characteristics of the male ego. Now it's time to "type" the male ego on the basis of a different attribute—his inherited personality style.

Our egos are molded and influenced by a variety of factors. That much has been established already. When we speak of the male ego, we refer to those factors that influence and mold the egos of a large proportion of the male population. In other words, we're generalizing about all (or most) men. That's what we do when we say "all men are . . ." or "all women are. . . ."

But in actuality, while men share much in common with each other (as do women) striking ego differences among different men do exist.

Some men are the very stereotypes of what we call "masculinity." Everything they do falls into that category. Other men seem to run completely counter to our conception of what a man should do or be like. Many men, perhaps the majority, fall in between: they have areas of "unmasculinity," but are for the most part quite masculine.

Personality obviously influences a person's ego development. The traits we possess determine at least in part the way we see ourselves, the way other people see us, our level of self-esteem, and the paths we take on our quest for a satisfied ego. By "typing" male personalities, we get a general idea of the "ego styles" that are distributed among the men we know.

It would be difficult to cover adequately all the approaches to personality that you find in the professional literature. Every personality theorist has his own idea about how you classify and understand the human personality.

But within the complex maze of personality theories, one approach stands out as having more support from scientific research than the others: the four temperament model first identified by Hippocrates, and later given scientific support by the British psychologist Hans Eysenck.[1]

According to Dr. Eysenck's research, two personality dimensions have a very strong impact upon our personality type: introversion/extroversion and general emotional drive. Whether we are more introverted or extroverted (or somewhere in between) depends upon how our central nervous system (brain) is constructed, while our level of emotionality is shaped by our autonomic nervous system. Both of those dimensions are strongly influenced by heredity.

The two dimensions of personality can be combined to form a graph, pictured below. Each quadrant of the graph represents a "personality type."

In other words, the combination of introversion-extroversion with the level of emotionality yields a personality type. Men who combine introversion with low emotionality would probably best be described as "easygoing." Those who are introverted and have a high level of emotionality are called "sensitive." Men who are ex-

Different Types of Men, Different Egos

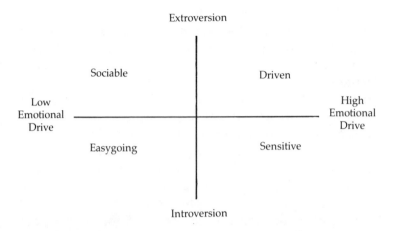

Extroversion

Sociable   Driven

Low   High
Emotional ——————|—————— Emotional
Drive   Drive

Easygoing   Sensitive

Introversion

troverted and highly emotional are "driven." And those who are extroverted and emotionally tame are "sociable."

Each of these four labels—easygoing, sensitive, driven, and sociable—represents a trait that seems *most characteristic* of those men. Actually, many more traits than those show up in each personality. A sensitive man, for example, will also display anxiety, creativity, and a wealth of other attributes. A driven man will likewise be extremely task-orientated, insensitive, domineering, and manipulative. These two types of men—the sensitive and the driven—will probably create the most ego problems for their women, at least in the usual sense of the word "ego."

A few words about the above graph are in order before we describe the four personality types and their corresponding ego styles in depth. First, keep in mind that although the process of describing personality in terms of "types" can be very illuminating and informative, it can also be harmful if it's carried to an extreme or if certain qualifications aren't recognized.

One such qualification is that the four "types" are generalizations or abstractions, based on descriptions of large samples of men who fall into each quadrant. In other words, we look at a lot of men who score alike and ask, "How are they similar to each other?" We don't emphasize how different men with the same basic personalities may be, and thus we run the risk of forcing all men into the same mold. So keep in mind that the descriptions are loose generalizations, not rigid categories.

Another qualification applies to men who do not fall strongly into one category or another. Some men are not strongly introverted or extroverted; they fall in the middle (we might call them ambiverts). Their personalities will be harder to describe than those of men who are more definitely introverts or extroverts. The same applies to men who score in the average range on a test of emotional drive.

But keeping those qualifications in mind, we can still use this information about personality types to understand one another better and to find ways of getting along better with different men. These personality types can yield warnings about weak areas that we need to improve. And they can help us discover ways to deal with ego problems.

The Easygoing Male

Men who combine introversion with low emotional drive are often described with such terms as easygoing, good-natured, or accommodating. As those terms imply, easygoing men are usually well-liked, pleasant people to be around.

Their low level of emotional drive prevents them from being pushy or overaggressive, even if they are in jobs where those traits are commonly found (salesman, for example), and their introverted tendencies lend an element of shyness and reserve to their personalities that some people find very attractive.

Some of the traits that we often find among easygoing men are as follows:

Flexibility. Easygoing men are usually able to adapt to a variety of different circumstances and people. They tend to be naturally accommodating. When there is conflict they adjust by suffering "the slings and arrows of outrageous fortune," as Shakespeare put it, instead of taking "arms against a sea of troubles." In other words, they more often simply accept bad circumstances rather than actively attempting to change them.

Peacemakers. Easygoing men detest strife and conflict, and crave peace and harmony. In marriage and at work they typically adopt a "peace-at-any-price" strategy and often devote their energies to diplomatic and peace-keeping initiatives. This sometimes causes them to yield too often and too readily on points of principle. As parents, they sometimes acquire reputations as the one who gives in, the "easy mark."

Even-tempered. Men who fall into the easygoing category generally have very even-tempered dispositions. They don't usually become manic or depressed (unless their relationship with a woman is disrupted). They seem for the most part to be stable and predictable. Extremely introverted men in this category are usually somewhat withdrawn while more ambiverted men are

[43]

more sociable. But both groups have a very pleasant disposition.

Patient. Because of their easygoing natures, these men are usually very patient. In families, they tend to have a very positive influence upon children—often spending hours with their young ones. At work, they often go in for activities that require patient concentration—mathematics and mechanics, for example.

Gentle. Easygoing men are usually very gentle with other people's egos, their wives included. We knew one easygoing man whose wife found sexual intercourse extremely painful. During their first year of marriage, they made love only twice. Despite his dissatisfaction with her sexual response, he was very gentle and patient with her; he spent hours holding and reassuring her. She finally had the problem surgically corrected, and they were able to enjoy a normal sex life. But I still remember his incredible patience and gentleness during that trying period in their marriage.

The easygoing man is generally very monogamous. He attaches strongly to one woman and maintains a very respectful, even worshipful, love for her. At times he seems highly dependent on her.

Under this sort of treatment, the wife often feels pampered and special. She is comfortable and secure with him, and usually is able to avoid many of the ego problems that men with other temperaments create for their wives.

Often women, particularly those with domineering, demanding husbands, long for a gentle, easygoing man. When the strain of living with an aggressive "go-getter" or a moody introvert gets a little hard to take, they find it very tempting to look enviously at Sue's husband, who is so considerate, and Jill's man, who goes along with all her desires and plans. "I just wish Jack could be more like Cindy's husband," they might think. "He treats her like a queen. Why, I've seen her order him around and totally ignore his feelings, and he still thinks she's the greatest woman on earth. He'd do *anything* for her!"

I counseled a young woman recently whose husband was "going off the deep end." He had always been a loving, committed mate, an excellent provider, and a good father to their three children. But lately he wanted to spend almost every night out with the boys and had become oblivious to her needs while still demanding that his own needs be met. Whenever his wife opposed his new behavior, he would get indignant and storm out of the house. Her life, as you can imagine, was in turmoil.

The worse her home life became, the more she thought about an old high-school boyfriend who had treated her almost too well. He had catered to her every wish and had adored her no matter what her mood or disposition. She thought about how pleasant their dates had been—no arguments over what to do—he always took her where she wanted to go; no demands or moodiness, he was happy just to be with her. She soon had conjured up an idealistic picture of how wonderful life would have been if she had just stayed with her old beau.

Many women do find easygoing men very attractive. Their kindness, gentleness, and patience seem to make them ideal mates. But let's take a closer look at these men, because their very strengths can, in some instances, become their worst weaknesses. In spite of their accommodating personalities, they sometimes have very bad luck with women; in fact, in some ways they present their women with as many problems as other men with more obvious ego weaknesses.

To the dismay of their friends and family, many of these kind and considerate men end up marrying ambitious, energetic, driving women. This was the case with Sal. He fell in love with Becky, a young woman determined to rise above her lower class background. While Sal enjoyed his relaxed, contented lifestyle, Becky was obsessed with bettering herself. She worked long, hard hours to advance in her job; she saved money diligently so she and Sal could buy a nice home; whenever possible she made social contact with the "right people" to assist her in her climb to the top.

Unfortunately Sal could not understand or adapt to her ambitiousness. His easygoing, winning ways, which Becky had found so attractive, carried over into his working style. Though Becky pushed, coaxed, threatened, and even ridiculed Sal for his lack of advancement at work, he was happy with his job and had no interest in seeking a promotion. Eventually Becky became so frustrated with Sal's lackadaisical attitude at work that she lost respect for him altogether. The traits of gentleness and contentment that she had once loved in Sal now repulsed her. They remained married because of the children, but intimacy left their relationship.

Of course, not all easygoing men are like Sal. Many of them do quite well in their jobs, advancing to prestigious and high-salaried positions. But even career success and a pleasing personality do not always spell happiness for these men and their wives.

Dick was the oldest of three boys. As a youngster he

enjoyed playing the bully with his younger brothers and their friends. But his mother, a compulsive woman who felt intimidated by aggressive men, decided that no son of hers would show this kind of hostility. She punished him severely, often breaking wooden spoons or paddles as she hit him. When beatings were socially inappropriate, she controlled his behavior by squeezing the back of his neck or by pinching him.

As Dick entered adolescence, he realized that he was a late maturer; nearly all his friends were surpassing him in strength and physical size. This, combined with his mother's oppressive discipline, undermined his confidence and prevented him from dating. Once he reached college age and attained normal stature, however, he regained his confidence and assertiveness with men, but was still shy and unaggressive around women.

At college Dick met his future wife, Jackie. She reminded Dick a lot of his mom, and he soon discovered that he was falling in love with her. They dated steadily, and everything went well as long as Dick accepted Jackie's strong-willed personality, giving in to her demands and asking little in return. But one day he stood up to her, and they got into an argument that ended up in a physical fight. Jackie kicked and clawed Dick; he couldn't believe the depth of hostility in the woman he loved. He broke up with her for a while, but something kept telling him, "This is the girl for me."

Eventually Dick and Jackie started dating again. Right after they finished college, they got married and both began working. Dick moved up quickly in his career; Jackie did well at her job, too, until she became pregnant and quit work to stay home with their daughter. On the surface everything seemed to be going well for Dick and Jackie: their marriage was strong; Dick was a devoted father and a good provider. But there were tell-tale signs of trouble ahead. Every now and then Jackie would snap at Dick, talking to him like a child, "Now listen here, Dick Williams . . ." and Dick would invariably take this treatment without a word of rebuke. It didn't even seem to bother him.

As Dick's daughter grew older, she adopted her mother's methods of relating to him. I remember once when I was at a ski party with the whole family. Jackie and the daughter stayed at the house to prepare supper while Dick and some friends went out on the lake for skiing. When supper was ready, the daughter marched out to the end of the dock and ordered Dick to shore. "Dick Williams, you get back here right now." To everyone's amazement, Dick didn't even correct her.

Dick loved his wife and daughter deeply and expressed his love by indulging them materially. He left his promising career to open his own business, working days, nights, and weekends to make it a success. His business really prospered, but Dick had to make more and more money to pay for Jackie's many wants.

Unfortunately, Dick's business kept him away from home for longer and longer periods of time. Jackie eventually got disgusted with his absence and decided that if Dick was going to work night and day, at least she should have something fabulous to show for his efforts. She announced to Dick one evening that she wanted him to buy her an airplane and give her flying lessons. This was too much for Dick and he finally refused to give in to her desires. A violent argument followed, in which Jackie detailed many complaints and resentments against Dick that she'd had for years. As a final blow she packed her bags and left Dick, never to return.

Dick suffered great hurt and despair when Jackie left. He had done everything humanly possible to make her happy. He had put up with her sharp tongue on numerous occasions without ever saying a word of rebuke. He had endured disrespect from his own daughter because he knew that criticizing her would upset Jackie. He had worked night and day to make his business a success so that his family's every desire could be fulfilled. Now all he had left was an empty house and a big alimony and child support payment each month.

Dick thought that by displaying patience, tenderness, love, and forbearance, he could soften Jackie's heart and retain her love. Unfortunately, by also accepting all her abusive treatment without a word, he failed to gain her respect. She felt that she could treat Dick any way at all—usually badly—and he would keep coming back for more. Dick, with all his admirable character traits, expected no growth or increasing maturity from Jackie, so she displayed none.

Dick's situation is sadly typical of many easygoing men. Women who are not married to them find them very attractive and desirable. But often their wives don't respect them a great deal. Whether this is true because women don't respect men who give in to them too much or because easygoing men tend to marry disrespectful women is not clear. But one thing is certain: an easygoing nature has its limitations and drawbacks just as do the other personality styles.

On the positive side, men with easygoing natures can display really saintly characters, even in the face of dreadful circumstances. I met a man several years ago who was a modern-day Hosea. You will recall that the Bible prophet Hosea's marriage was a symbol of Israel's relationship with God: "The Lord said to Hosea, 'Go and marry a girl who is a prostitute. . . . This will illustrate the way my people have been untrue to me . . .'" (Hos. 1:2 TLB). So Hosea married Gomer, a harlot, who continued her immoral lifestyle even after her marriage and the birth of several children.

Despite Gomer's degrading behavior, Hosea (representing God's love) continued to love her: "I will court her again, and bring her into the wilderness, and speak to her tenderly there" (Hos. 2:14 TLB). Even after Gomer left home to pursue adulterous affairs, God told Hosea, "'Go, and get your wife again and bring her back to you and love her, even though she loves adultery'" (Hos. 3:1 TLB).

I could never imagine Hosea's actually *loving* Gomer after she had treated him so shamefully. But then I met Doug. He was a handsome, successful businessman who exuded quiet charm and warmth. Everyone who worked under his supervision, men and women alike, had the highest regard for him. Whenever his name came up in conversation, someone would remark about what a wonderful guy he was, how easygoing and kind. In fact, he was so over-endowed with positive traits that he seemed too good to be true.

Doug could have had any woman he wanted as a wife, but for some reason he married Joyce, a young woman of questionable character. His high moral standards so contrasted with her lower ones that their early years of marriage were stormy and ridden with conflict. Joyce still sought the attention of other men while Doug remained loyally devoted to her. She left him to live with another man for awhile, but when her lover rejected her, Joyce returned to Doug, who gladly accepted her back.

Their marriage stabilized temporarily, but soon Joyce was dating other men again. Through it all Doug remained loyal to Joyce and continued to love her. Although he never mentioned her wayward behavior directly, I once heard him say that people should take the position God takes toward us: we should love and accept others no matter what they have done in the past or even continue to do. He stressed forgiveness and reconciliation instead of censure and separation.

It takes an easygoing man, a gentle, kind, and patient man to display forgiveness and devotion to a wife who repeatedly breaks her marriage vows. It also takes a special woman to truly appreciate the strengths of an easygoing man without taking advantage of them. She will have to accept responsibility for curbing her own negative tendencies, since her man will be unlikely to point them out or push for her to correct them. Since the easygoing man will probably idolize her to some extent, she will have to maintain a humble attitude to avoid the pitfalls of self-righteousness. But a woman who can face up to her own limitations and set out to overcome them can find much happiness and contentment with an easygoing man.

There is one area that gives particular trouble to the easygoing man—he hates conflict and confrontation. He is a peace-at-any-price person, and sometimes the price he has to pay for harmony is very high. Sal lost the respect of his wife, Dick lost his family, and Doug lost at least some of his self-respect as well as the sanctity of his marriage.

[51]

Occasionally the easygoing man may also find himself losing control over his children. He is generally an excellent father—kind, patient, deeply concerned for the welfare of his children, and able to relate well to children on their own level. We knew an easygoing man several years ago who was a modern-day pied piper. Wherever he went, children would flock to him. He told them secrets, had a "cricket" (his fingers rubbing together) chirp in their ears, led them around the yard playing follow the leader. He was also able to discipline the children if they needed it.

But some easygoing men dislike conflict so much that they allow their children to take over the household. They love to play with the kids, to have heart-to-heart talks with them; but if the kids get out of line or make unreasonable demands, these men can't handle the confrontation necessary to set things straight. Ernie had this problem. He was a quiet, likeable fellow who just wanted to get along with everybody else. He found it easier to give in to his children's desires than to create a scene.

Ernie's children were just toddlers when they learned how to manipulate their parents. They generally would ask their mom for whatever they wanted. If she said yes, then everything was fine. If she said no, they went immediately to Ernie for a second opinion. Usually Ernie said yes, just because it was so much easier to keep them happy that way. But occasionally, especially when his wife had jumped on him about being such a pushover, Ernie would say no. Then the children would go into strategy number three. They cried, begged, screamed, threw themselves on the floor—whatever was necessary to make Ernie give in. And give in he did;

it was just a matter of how long it took before the children wore him down.

Ernie and his wife eventually came to me for counseling. Their children were having trouble in school and had been expelled several times. They lacked respect for all authority and were sources of continual problems for their teachers and principal. Fortunately, when Ernie realized how his peace-at-any-price strategy was hurting his family, he felt highly motivated to learn effective means of confrontation. Within a few months he and his wife began to present a united front to the children, and a deeper harmony came to the home. The children's school problems gradually cleared up, too.

The Sensitive Man

Sensitive men combine introversion with a high level of emotional drive. The introversion makes them somewhat shy, withdrawn, and unsociable while the high emotional drive creates a tendency toward general anxiety. The result is a man who is very emotionally sensitive. Specifically, those two dimensions predispose the sensitive man toward the following attributes:

Social anxiety. The sensitive man's most enduring and unpleasant experience is a fear of social situations and interchanges. Above all, he fears rejection and will do anything to avoid it. This fear creates all sorts of social problems for him, such as hesitancy to initiate contacts with women, shyness at work, and fear of asking for a raise. The hypersensitivity to rejection also encourages these men to become suspicious of other people and to employ a variety of testing maneuvers in order to see if others will reject or accept them.

Sometimes the sensitive man dreams of dating beautiful women, of being the envy of the entire room as he walks in with a gorgeous girl beside him. But frequently reality finds him very uncomfortable and anxious around good-looking women, if he should happen to be in their presence. In fact, he is often so inhibited and lacking in self-confidence that he won't ask women out at all; they must ask him out first.

When the sensitive man falls in love, he still fears rejection from his woman. He remains alert for signs of her waning interest in him, all the time desiring that he be the object of her total devotion. If their relationship looks like it will be a permanent one, the sensitive man has a hard time setting the date for their marriage. Jan thought she would grow old waiting for Larry to decide on the date of their marriage. She thought about the millions of married couples around the world and wondered, "Was it *this* hard for all of them to make the final commitment?"

Finally Jan offered Larry an ultimatum. She was graduating from college, and either he would have to set a date for the wedding or she would take a job out of town. Larry realized that he had postponed the inevitable as long as he could and promptly told Jan they could get married in six weeks! She had to dash around making all the arrangements for a church wedding, but they were married on schedule and have had a very happy marriage since then.

Sometimes things don't work out as well as they did for Larry. If a sensitive man's worst fears come true, if he is rejected by the woman he loves, it can be an ego-crushing experience for him. George had loved Betsy for almost as long as he could remember. They had attended the same church since childhood, and he had always found her beautiful. They started dating in high school and were talking seriously about marriage when Betsy had to go away for the summer. George wrote her long letters telling of his great love for her, but Betsy's letters became more and more "friendly" rather than loving. When she returned home, George discovered that Betsy had met someone else. But rather than give up his love, he inwardly clung to it, always hoping that Betsy's old feelings would return. He never dated anyone else; he just couldn't face being hurt like that again. Several years later, after Betsy had moved out of town, he began writing her again and even traveled five hundred miles to see her in the hope that their old love could be rekindled. Unfortunately, Betsy cared for him deeply as a friend, but she just did not love him. Even after Betsy married someone else, George rarely dated and did not get married himself until he was thirty-five years old. His mother once remarked, "I don't think George has ever gotten over Betsy's rejection of him."

Moodiness. When high emotional drive combines with introversion, a moody disposition usually results. Sensitive men rarely have extreme highs, but they are very prone to having emotional lows, especially after they have been rejected.

Conscientiousness. The sensitive man often has a very detail-oriented mind. He can usually concentrate on one topic for long periods of time, and thus comes to see it from all angles. This detail orientation makes it likely that he will be conscientious and at least a little compulsive; thus, he may be good in math, computer science, and other "detail" fields. He may also be very critical of others—alert to their flaws, in other words. He may be a perfectionist—making it hard for him to live with others and with himself.

Low self-confidence. A sensitive man is the most likely of all types to have low self-esteem and a lack of self-confidence. His mood swings make it hard for him to trust himself. His fear of rejection discourages him from feeling good about his relationships with other people and creates in him a pervasive sense of helplessness. In order to feel good about himself, the sensitive man often has to succeed in areas that don't require him to interact with groups of people. But in order to succeed, he also has to overcome his own negative feelings about himself.

Danny had always been intelligent and creative, but one wouldn't have known it by his school grades. He rarely passed his subjects, not because he couldn't grasp the material, but because he was always too upset by family turmoil and low self-esteem to concentrate on schoolwork. Despite his low grades, however, Danny managed to get into college because of high scores on aptitude tests. But his grades were no better there than in high school until he made a dramatic break from his old life and moved away from home. Once he was on his own, Danny's confidence in himself and his abilities increased dramatically. He learned new study habits and began to achieve outstanding success in his classes. He decided that he wanted to study aerospace engineering and eventually got accepted into one of the best schools in the country.

Once Danny got his life turned around, once he gained that determination and self-confidence he had always needed, he worked almost fanatically to prevent a return to his old patterns. He finally graduated at the top of his class, to the great amazement of his old friends and family. His fear of falling back into old patterns of failure and low self-esteem motivated him to excel.

Unfortunately, not all sensitive men have this self-confidence or this drive to succeed. Sometimes past failure can lead to paralyzing fear that prevents them from attempting anything worthwhile. I counseled a secretary recently whose husband had been out of work for seven months. He was becoming more and more lethargic and depressed, resisting all her attempts to encourage and motivate him. She related this story to me.

Her husband had had a good job with an auto parts company, a position that was both challenging and emotionally satisfying. Everything seemed to be going well at home, too; but then the economy sagged, and the auto industry was the first to suffer. The auto parts company went out of business with almost no advance warning, and the secretary's husband was out of work. At first he spent every day looking for a job, but soon she noticed a disturbing pattern emerging in his behavior. He looked diligently through the want ads for job openings and asked all his friends for possible leads. But whenever he discovered a job opening, he postponed applying for the position until it was already filled. The secretary soon realized that he feared rejection so much that he just couldn't bring himself to apply for a job. He preferred to remain unemployed rather than face the hurt of having his application turned down.

Although the sensitive man usually reacts in one of two ways when he fears failure—either redoubling his efforts to avoid the failure or not trying, thus eliminating the possibility of failure or success—occasionally a sensitive man will choose a third alternative; that of setting unrealistic goals. He will set out to accomplish a task so difficult that no one in his right mind would attempt it; then when he fails, no one can look down on him.

I had a graduate student who adopted this behavior pattern. He was having problems finishing his dissertation; and when I talked with him about possible ways to complete his work, he decided to embark on a totally new topic, one much more difficult than his previous one. After a few weeks of trying without success to get him started on his new topic, I suggested he return to his original study. Once again he decided to change topics, this time choosing a research project that was totally beyond his reach both financially and technically. Eventually he had to abandon his dissertation altogether, taking a few months off to work and save money. But somehow his ego remained more or less intact through the experience. He reasoned, "Well, I shouldn't feel so bad that I couldn't complete my dissertation. After all, I chose a really monumental study. I didn't do it, but none of my classmates could have either." This seemed to appease his ego and distract him from the real issue: other students chose reasonable topics and completed them; he chose unreasonable studies and never completed anything.

Cautiousness. Just as the sensitive man is extremely cautious about making the permanent commitment to marriage, he may also find it difficult to decide to have a child. In this case, he doesn't usually fear failure; he fears losing control over his life. Having a child means a big adjustment in lifestyle; but more critically for the sensitive man, it can mean an inability to determine exactly how his life will proceed. After all, there are many unknowns in having a child. Will it be a boy or a girl? Will it be healthy? Will it be intelligent? Will I be able to relate to the new baby? Will I love him/her? Will the baby affect the relationship between me and my wife? For the sensitive man who likes everything nailed down, planned out, and under control, these uncertainties can stir up great anxiety.

I counseled a couple recently in which the husband was an extremely sensitive man who liked to have his life well planned. Glenn had told Rosemary about his long-term "strategy" even before they married. He planned for both of them to work and save as much money as possible for three years. Then they would buy a home. Five years later, they would buy a new car. His whole scheme depended on both of them working full time throughout their marriage.

Well, Rosemary got pregnant, an event that Glenn was totally unprepared for. When she told him, Glenn was furious and panicked at the same time. He demanded that she get an abortion, but she just couldn't accept that as a reasonable alternative. So they came to see me for counseling. I explained to Glenn that his feelings were fairly typical of men expecting their first child, especially an unplanned one, and that he would soon feel more comfortable with the idea of being a parent. He seemed unconvinced; so Rosemary, in an effort to make him feel better, offered, "I'll go back to work if you want me to. . . ." Glenn then tried a new strategy—martyrdom. "Don't worry about it," he told her. "I'm used to having my plans disrupted." He sat in my office with his head in his hands, trying every maneuver he could think of to keep Rosemary from having a baby.

Fortunately for them, time is a great healer of wounds and anxiety. I saw Rosemary several weeks later, and she told me that Glenn, after the initial panic, had made a 180 degree turn. He was now actually looking forward to being a parent and had agreed to be in the delivery room with her when the baby was born.

Creativity. One of the sensitive man's greatest strengths is his creative drive. He is often able to see things from a fresh angle and to produce new and original insight. The same sensitivity that makes him fear social rejection also enables this man to become attuned to nuances and subtle perceptions. The high emotional drive provides a source of energy that finds its most satisfying outlet in creative endeavors. Many of the world's inventors, artists, writers, and philosophers have had this personality type.

From a woman's standpoint, one of the most difficult ego problems that the sensitive man's wife has to face is his moodiness. Sensitive men can place great emotional demands on their women; and for that reason they usually choose as wives women who are cheerful, upbeat, easygoing, and emotionally stable. Like most married men (and women), they look toward their spouses for the thing they lack, and the most obvious thing they lack is an even-tempered disposition.

One of our friends, Joe Morris, fits this pattern. His emotional sensitivity lends an important impetus to his work as an artist. He is very creative and perceptive, and commands much respect for his innovative ideas.

In part, that's what attracted Kathy, his fiancée, to Joe. She liked his sensitivity and his status as a "boy genius." There were signs of moodiness during the courtship, but both were so energized by their love for each other that they stayed for the most part on an emotional high.

After a few months of marriage, however, problems began to surface. Joe demonstrated some of the moodiness at home that had been absent during their courtship. Kathy would become agitated whenever Joe went into one of his "blue funks." She took his mood swings as a comment on her importance to him (always a dangerous reaction to a moody person). Her self-esteem was lowered and she felt on the defensive. As she withdrew from him, he became even moodier and began to attack her. A vicious cycle was started that was extremely difficult to break.

Fortunately they did eventually break that cycle, though. The breakthrough came when Kathy realized that Joe's moods were not her fault. As she stopped withdrawing and instead began to give him emotional support, Joe's mood swings seemed to end more quickly. Kathy also found that she could stop Joe from criticizing her by simply describing her feelings to him. "Joe, it really makes me feel hurt when you pick at my housecleaning," she would say, instead of defending herself or attacking him back. Joe, ever sensitive to Kathy's expressions of feelings, would respond by becoming more supportive himself.

The same sensitivity that makes these men react so strongly to negative events or criticism also helps them to experience empathy for other people's feelings. Often their women can help them act more kindly simply by describing how they feel when criticized or put down.

The Happy-go-lucky Man

Happy-go-lucky men are usually extroverts in the typical sense of the word. They are delightful to be around, especially in social situations, and they quickly

make new friends. In a sense, they are the exact opposites of sensitive men.

Happy-go-lucky men combine extroversion with a
low level of emotional drive. They are friendly and fun-
loving, relaxed with themselves and at peace with the
world. Few worries cloud their sunny horizon. Lacking
the determination that comes from a high level of emotional drive, they find it easy to flit from one project to
another without an organizing plan to give their activities coherence. Their extroverted nature causes these
men to be somewhat easily distracted anyway, and the
low emotionality lends an easygoing, upbeat manner to
their behavior. Specifically, happy-go-lucky men generally display the following attributes.

Sociability. Happy-go-lucky men are the most outgoing and sociable of the four types. They enjoy meeting,
being around, and talking with people. Easygoing men
and, to a lesser extent, sensitive men, may also like people; but they generally prefer to be with one person at a
time. Not so with the happy-go-lucky man. The more
the merrier. He thrives in groups.

I knew a minister who was the epitome of the happy-
go-lucky man. He was so at ease with himself and large
groups of people that the first time he ever spoke at our
church, he told the entire congregation about the death
of his first wife, his subsequent remarriage, and his two
sets of children. He made everyone feel comfortable
with him while he put to rest all questions that would
inevitably have arisen over the fact that he had four children very close in age with two sets of last names.

Recently this minister had his sixty-second birthday,
and his congregation gave a party for him. Knowing
how much he loved people (and lots of them), they in-

vited members of his former congregations. People came from as far as a hundred miles away, packing the church and bringing dozens of dishes for a potluck supper after church. The minister was in his glory, surrounded by friends and family. He didn't even mind blowing out sixty-two candles: "You know how much the kids love candles," he said.

Because he often goes for quantity rather than quality in his social relationships, the happy-go-lucky man is sometimes described as superficial. He does tend to be inconsistent in his relationships with people. He may be so enthusiastic that a person comes to believe that he is a best friend. That person could be disappointed later, for the happy-go-lucky man tends to think only about the people he's with at the time. The next time you see him, he may hardly know you.

He also enthusiastically accepts any social invitation; he's in his glory at such gatherings. But when the time comes to attend, he may forget the event or show up late.

I once attended a week-of-prayer service and was delighted to discover that the speaker was a pastor from my youth, a dynamic, energetic speaker with a real message to deliver. After the service I went up to talk with him, and he greeted me like a long-lost friend. We talked a lot about old times and had a wonderful visit together. Since he was staying in a camper and eating at the school cafeteria, I invited him to eat with my family two nights later; he accepted graciously and eagerly, saying he'd "really enjoy a home-cooked meal." All the arrangements were made, and we went our separate ways.

On the appointed evening I went to his camper to

pick him up, and he was nowhere to be seen. I waited about forty-five minutes, and he finally showed up, looking somewhat surprised to see me. But he recovered quickly, and we went to my house. Apparently he had already eaten supper, because he barely touched his food that night. Nevertheless, he showed no signs of embarrassment and spent the rest of the evening sharing stories with my whole family, thoroughly entertaining us all.

Disorganized. You can usually tell when an office is filled with people whose personalities fall into this category. The rooms will be buzzing with activity and talk; if there is a schedule, few people will be following it, and a general climate of disorganization will be evident. The workers will be so caught up in whatever is happening at the moment that they will have trouble making forward progress.

My wife worked in the same office with a happy-go-lucky man. He usually rushed in thirty seconds before time to begin work; otherwise he rushed in five minutes late. He spent nearly all day on the phone with clients, listening to their problems or helping them to understand the multitude of laws relating to the welfare system. He was always busy, busy, busy, stopping only long enough for lunch. Everyone in the office assumed he had his work well under control. But when he left to take another job, his supervisor discovered that his caseload was in complete disarray. He had spent so much time conversing with his clients, helping them the best way he knew, that he had failed to do the essential paperwork. It took three workers almost a month to straighten out the mess he left behind.

The happy-go-lucky man is often described with such

terms as "scatterbrained" or "easily distracted." The worst television interview I ever took part in was conducted by a man whose personality was in this category. It was an extremely confusing and frustrating experience, as he hopped from one topic to the next without any connecting theme. This contrasted sharply with another interview conducted by an easygoing man. It was slow, organized, and easy to follow.

Cheerfulness. One of the most attractive features of the happy-go-lucky man's personality is his upbeat nature. His cheerfulness and vivaciousness are infectious, and other people feel good just to be around him. These men enjoy living, and they can very readily bring a feeling of excitement into the lives of other people.

A happy-go-lucky friend of mine teaches a women's exercise class. He started it to make a few extra dollars, not expecting much because his group was so small. But because his enthusiasm and cheerfulness were so contagious, the group quickly began to grow. Soon they had to move to a larger facility and divide the class into two sessions. Even when the women are exhausted from their work-out and straining to get that last exercise in, his energy and zest keep them going.

A drawback to this type of personality is the temptation these men face to get by solely on their charm and cheerfulness. As children, they learn quickly how to please their parents, and often less is demanded of them than of their siblings. This often aggravates their irresponsible tendencies.

I have talked with many parents who have one happy-go-lucky child and another with a somewhat less cheerful disposition. "I can't believe how aggravated I get at Mark!" their comments typically go. "If I ask him to take out the trash, he grumbles, argues, and goes into slow motion. Oh, yes, he eventually gets the job done, but by then I feel as though I've been dragged through the mud. Now, Michael, that's a different story. If I ask him to pick up his toys, he just smiles and says, 'Okay, Mommy!' He makes me feel so good. He doesn't always follow through with the work, but he's so delightful I hate to punish him. . . ."

Impulsiveness. On almost any test of introversion/extroversion you'll find the following item: "I often speak and act on the spur of the moment." This is an extrovert item. Almost all extroverts check it, and it applies most of all to the emotionally stable extrovert. Their extroversion causes them to be "sharers" or "doers." And their stable emotions render them so relaxed and easygoing that they don't worry about what they say or do. These are the men who will get in a group and "let it all hang out," telling incidents from the past or present that, according to their family or friends, might be better left untold.

The happy-go-lucky man is easily caught up in his surroundings. As those surroundings change, he changes. If his peers are using drugs, he uses drugs; if dirty jokes are being told, he joins right in, despite any convictions against the practice. This sort of accommodating impulsiveness characterizes the happy-go-lucky man, as opposed to the initiatory impulsiveness that typifies the driven man. I'll never forget a weekend I spent with Jack and several of our mutual friends.

Jack and his wife were separated, and he was enjoying the carefree life of a traveling salesman. He met people everywhere and thoroughly enjoyed being with each one of them. When he got to the cabin where we were staying, he was on a "people-high." He had enjoyed his week so much that he hadn't given his wife a second thought. But once he got to our retreat and things settled down, he started to feel very bad about the strained relationship between him and his wife. He spent over two hours talking with a counselor, reading the Bible, and praying; then he called his wife long-distance to attempt a reconciliation. He told her how much he loved her—that he was a changed man. At the end of the weekend, he was sincerely sorry for his part in the breakup and was determined to make his marriage work, no matter how hard that might be.

Unfortunately, his enthusiasm lasted only until he got around a different group of friends. He felt strongly about returning to his wife while he was with us and equally strongly about having a good time when he was with them.

The Driven Man

The driven man is one who combines extroversion with high emotional drive. Research indicates that high emotional drive has a different effect upon the personalities of introverts and extroverts. Since introverts have less self-confidence, they experience high emotional drive as anxiety and fearfulness. When the introvert is emotionally activated, he generally feels agitated, excited, or high-strung.

Unlike introverts, extroverts experience emotional activation as an energizing force that increases their drive level, self-confidence, and initiative. If the emotional drive gets too high, they become manic and grandiose in their aspirations and plans. They may become like

[67]

Hitler or Napoleon, ready to conquer the world and set up their empire no matter what the cost. If it stays on a more moderate level, they will simply be very active and driven, striving relentlessly to achieve success.

I recently talked to the wife of a driven man who had taken a failing business and made it a tremendous success through sheer hard work and determination. She told me, "I'm convinced that Reg would have made a success out of anything he tried to do. I saw him take that trucking company, which was near bankruptcy, and turn it completely around. Even though he knew almost nothing about trucking when he bought the business, he worked twelve to fourteen hours a day and then came home at night and studied books on how to make a success of his company. Many times he worked around the clock to keep the trucks running on schedule."

This high drive-level seems central to men with this personality type. Other characteristics include:

Insensitivity. These are the sort of men who "ride roughshod over the feelings of others" as they try to reach their own goals. Under the promptings of high emotional drive, these men simply don't give much attention to such minor details as other people's feelings. They may drive their employees with the same fervor with which they push themselves. They may expect them to work long (and indefinite) hours in less-than-desirable conditions and then express shock and dismay when the employees complain. Sometimes their insensitivity to others' needs runs so deep that they are unable to keep workers for more than a few months at a time. But that does not bother them. They just work that much harder and become that much more determined to succeed.

Often the family life suffers as the wife and children of the driven man feel neglected and/or abused. The demanding insensitivity that causes his employees so many problems also hurts the family of the driven man. He expects everyone, especially those close to him, to have the same drive, the same will to succeed that he possesses. If they don't, he can become harsh and critical. He may berate his wife for failing to keep the house spotless and cook gourmet meals, even if she works a full-time job besides rearing several children. He may stand over his children and watch them like a prison guard as they try to improve their less-than-perfect grades. If he tries to help them with their homework, his severe and overbearing manner may make them so nervous that they do worse instead of better, setting up a vicious cycle of failure—criticism—stress—failure.

Driven men are extroverts, but not in the usual sense of the word. They are outgoing in a blunt, sometimes arrogant way, as opposed to the easygoing, charming manner of the happy-go-lucky man. Driven men can be very charming, though, when charm is necessary to help them reach some goal. I worked with a man who was the perfect host the first time I went to his home. He made everyone feel at ease; he and his wife served the meal with great flair; he kept a lively and entertaining conversation going the entire evening. But I soon came to see another side of him. Once he had gained my friendship and admiration, he became arrogant, trying to gain an upper hand in our relationship by various subtle maneuvers. His warmth and charm proved to be a facade to entice people into his web of psychological domination.

Aggressiveness. Driven men can be counted on to throw themselves into their goals. Of all the personality types, these men are the most aggressive. Their emotional drive combines with their aggressive energy, and their insensitivity prevents them from worrying too much over how other people are going to respond to their actions.

If driven men are well socialized, they can be very productive. But if they are not well trained, they can easily become criminals and psychopaths. In fact, a large proportion of aggressive crime comes from men with this personality type.

Energetic. Driven men generally bubble over with energy. The happy-go-lucky man also appears very energetic, but his energy is mainly social—expressed as a joy in being with people. The driven man's energy is more goal-oriented and focused. He is not as likely to be distracted from what he wants as is the happy-go-lucky extrovert. Happy-go-lucky men and driven men will play baseball with strikingly different techniques. The cheerful man will expend a lot of energy just having fun. At a church baseball game recently, the pastor showed up in cut-off jeans, a T-shirt, and a floppy hat. (He is truly a joy-filled, happy man. I called his house several weeks ago, and he answered the phone so exuberantly that I stood there speechless for a second or two before I could say anything.) When the pastor made a hit, he ran toward first base with his arms waving wildly and yelling, "Look out everybody, here I come!" He amazed everyone with his boundless enthusiasm and zest for living. He didn't care whether his team won or lost—he was just out there to have a good time.

Out in left field, a driven man was displaying a completely different kind of energy. He stood poised and alert, watching intently every ball that was thrown and every hit that was made. If the ball came anywhere near his position, he took off to catch it and nearly always succeeded. He had a specific goal in mind—to do all in his power to help his team win—and he focused all his energy toward meeting that goal.

The sensitive man also has access to a high amount of emotional energy, but his pessimism and low self-esteem incline him to experience that energy as anxiety and moodiness. But the driven man has confidence in his abilities and optimism about his chances for success. His emotional energy is experienced as exuberance and enthusiasm.

Domination. Driven men are generally domineering. In social conversations they often talk quite a bit and determine the topic under discussion. Even if they are sociable, their conversation typically revolves around what they are doing—their new projects, goals, or interests.

These men are often overbearing in the home, directing their children's activities and keeping the household under control. If they also lack warmth, the children will grow up either cowed or rebellious. In fact, this type of personality is the most likely to produce rebelliousness at adolescence.

This personality type is also the most likely to have a "male ego problem" in the usual sense of the term. The sensitive man likes to be reassured often. But he is usually sensitive to his mate's needs in return. Not so the driven man. Unless he makes a strong effort to take his wife's needs into consideration, the driven man will be very demanding of her. He will want her to praise and support him, but he will give little praise and support in return.

[71]

Boldness. Driven men are usually bold and brazen. As children, they are often seen in child counseling agencies with a mother who complains, "I can't seem to do anything with him. Punishment doesn't work. He gets worse. He was always this way, from the moment of birth." One mother of a driven child told me about one episode (among many in her life) that seemed to capture the essence of what these mothers are up against.

"Will caused a real scene at supper last night. He refused to eat, and after my husband and I left the table, he started throwing mashed potatoes at his sisters. When I walked into the room and saw mashed potatoes all over the walls and the floor, I knew I had to take action. So I took Will to his bedroom, shut the door, and spanked him with a wooden spoon. He screamed and cried a lot, but didn't seem very repentant. In fact, when I told him to go to the kitchen and clean up the mess he had made, he refused. So I spanked him again and told him to stay in his room until he was ready to obey me. I didn't hear anything else from him that evening and just assumed that he had gone to sleep rather than come out and clean up the potatoes. But when I went in to check on him before I went to bed, I found that he systematically peeled pieces of his wallpaper off all four walls in his bedroom. He had put them in a neat pile by the door so I would be sure to see them when I entered the bedroom."

That boldness, which is so hard on mothers, helps driven men in business. They take calculated risks and aren't fearful of negative consequences.

FIVE

The Child Is Father of the Man

When I first met Janice, she felt confused, hurt, and frustrated. She had been dating Bob for almost a year and was deeply in love with him. He, in turn, had told her repeatedly of his love for her, but lately his actions left her painfully puzzled.

Janice had met Bob, a successful young lawyer, on a blind date, and they had felt a special attraction for each other right away. They dated each other exclusively for many months, and Janice felt certain that Bob's marriage proposal was just around the corner. Yet he didn't propose; instead he started dating other women one or two nights a week. Janice saw her dream world come crashing down. She became despondent, then angry. She confronted Bob, asking if he just wanted to break up their relationship. He assured her that he still loved her, but that he just wanted to date around a little. He also told her that he would prefer her not dating anyone else.

Janice didn't know what to do. Should she submit to Bob's seemingly unreasonable desire for loyalty from her while he dated other women? Wouldn't he lose respect for her if she did? Or should she protect herself and start cultivating new friendships? Would this drive Bob away and perhaps ruin the best relationship she'd ever had with a man? Janice was at a real crossroad in her life. She was thirty-two years old and afraid that the time in which she could have a family was rapidly passing. If she handled this situation correctly, she felt sure that one day she and Bob could have a happy life together. But if she chose the wrong course of action, she faced losing the man she loved.

Janice came to me for counseling and described the whole story in depth—the pain, the fears she felt, and above all the dilemma of how to react to Bob's unusual behavior. I asked her to tell me about Bob, and it was then that the whole situation began to make sense. She told me that Bob was the oldest child in his family and that he had a younger brother. Since I had done quite a bit of studying in the subject of birth order, this little piece of information told me enough to help Janice decide on her best course of action. We used our knowledge of family position to map out Janice's best reaction to Bob's behavior.

Janice and Bob stayed together, got married, and now have a happy and stable home with two young sons. The subject of birth order proved very crucial to their relationship, and it is one that will help almost any woman understand her man better.

Birth Order and the Male Ego

What does birth order have to do with the male ego? And what is birth order anyway?

Most of us grow up in families. Within those families we occupy one of four positions—oldest, middle, youngest, or only child. This is our birth order. Frequently it is helpful to break these categories down further, describing the other children in the family, too; thus, you may be the oldest child with younger brothers, oldest child with younger sisters, youngest child with older brothers, and so on.

Birth order, important as it is, also interacts with temperament and parental relationships to shape the male personality and ego. Two people with the same birth order position may be similar in many ways, but different in many other ways. What I offer here are general descriptions of the various family positions; they may fit your man exactly ("That's Harold! That's just like him!"), or they may just give you a few more clues to understand why he acts the way he does.

A child's role in his family helps to determine what roles he will seek and feel comfortable with in adulthood. Thus a first-born child who has to care for and take charge of younger children in the family will likely be a good provider and leader in his own family. A child who, from birth, grows up surrounded by older children and doesn't spend a lot of time interacting with adults, may feel more comfortable in a clique of peers, or working with other people, than by himself.

But birth order influences much more than our choice of roles in life. It can affect how we react to circumstances outside our control, how we relate to authority and moral values, how threatened we feel by the small and large problems of life. Our birth order can reach down to our very self-image and help determine what we think of ourselves and how we respond to what others think of us. It can also influence how we treat other people and what we expect of them.

Since this book deals with the male ego, I will cover

only the major male birth order positions. As you will soon see, a boy's position in his family can have far-reaching consequences in his manhood.

Firstborn Male

Parents await the arrival of their first child with an intense mixture of excitement and anxiety. Father and mother have been duly warned that "this will be a really big adjustment for you." Often first-time parents have examined all the latest theories on child-rearing and have spent many hours deciding just the right way to raise this very special child. They look forward to their child's birth with some strong opinions about the way a child should be trained, while at the same time they have little or no practical experience in the real issues of parenting.

The parents direct all this enthusiasm, all these strong opinions, all this insecurity and inexperience, toward one small infant. They expect him to out-perform, out-achieve, out-behave every other child that has ever been born. And frequently they are willing to expend the time and energy necessary to see that he does all these things.

We should not be surprised, therefore, to find that, in general, firstborn children are conscientious, responsible, conforming to parental standards, sometimes self-righteous, serious, emotionally dependent on others, and a little tense, anxious, and fearful. Their parents have put a lot of pressure on them to behave correctly, and they have complied, sometimes at the expense of spontaneity. But there is a strange paradox here. While firstborns generally follow rules and regulations outside the home, they are often engaged in angry confrontations with the parents, who live in bewilderment over this well-trained child who seems so stubborn and strong-willed. Many times this situation occurs because the parents have indeed trained the child well, maybe too well, and he is fighting for his individuality.

In school and later in the workplace, firstborns are high achievers—many become doctors, lawyers, college professors, or scientists. (Einstein, Newton, and Freud were all firstborns.) Unfortunately, a higher percentage of firstborns than people in other birth order positions commit or contemplate suicide, perhaps because they cannot live up to the expectations they have internalized from their parents.

Recently a man and his wife brought their thirteen-year-old daughter to me for counseling. She was almost a straight-A student, played the piano, kept her room immaculate, and had a wealth of friends. On top of that, she was well behaved and pretty. What was her problem? "She's too hard on herself," said her mother. "She cries if she gets a B in school, and lately she has been telling me that she doesn't think she'll live many more years." Both parents were understandably upset.

What was intriguing, though, was the difference between this over-socialized firstborn and her happy-go-lucky younger brother. He did poorly in school, never cleaned up his room (Mom always did it for him), and was so cheerful and happy that his parents seemed disinclined to burden him with responsibility. The parents in this family had done what many other parents had done. They spent so much time preparing their first child to be God's gift to the planet that when the second one came along, they said to themselves (unconsciously, of course), "Why don't we just relax and enjoy this one?" Hence the guilt-ridden, high achieving, unsatisfied first child and the relaxed, cheerful, scatterbrained later child. When they grow up, they have uniquely opposite sets of problems in marriages and social relationships.

Firstborns have the most problems getting along with people. They tend to be more introverted than those other birth order positions and show signs of compulsiveness—a need to order their world in a predictable way. This compulsiveness does not always lend itself to ease in social situations where spontaneity and flexibility are called for. These are not attributes in which firstborns specialize.

The Firstborn Male with Younger Brothers

When Janice told me about Bob's position as the oldest child with a younger brother, I described to her several characteristics that made Bob's strange behavior more understandable.

Of all birth order positions, this one expects the most of women without offering a lot in return. Since the oldest brother of brothers is not used to women (except his mother), he doesn't know how to act around them. If, during childhood, he tries hitting them on the arm or rough-housing as he does with his younger brother, he soon discovers that girls aren't especially appreciative of this treatment. He has to learn by trial and error how to act in the presence of girls. In addition, he is usually a high-achiever in school, but unfortunately many teenage girls are more interested in boys with athletic ability. So he's not what you would call a lady's man during adolescence.

The Child Is Father of the Man

But the funny thing is that although he may present a cool, controlled exterior around the opposite sex, *he will be thrilled when a girl shows interest in him.* This is a flattering experience for a young man who is not used to women. But flattering though it might be, to show too much enthusiasm for a girl would mean a loss of control; and oldest males love to be in control of everything in their environment, including themselves.

Once an oldest male reaches adulthood and begins to think seriously of marriage, he is very particular about what he wants in a wife and very cautious about entering into a relationship that invariably means losing some control. So it is difficult for him to make the final decision on getting married. As Bob's love for Janice grew stronger, he wanted more than ever to be sure he was making the right decision about proposing to her. He felt compelled to date other girls just to be certain Janice was the right wife for him; the maneuver also enabled him to regain more control over his life. What Janice saw as Bob's pulling away from their close relationship was merely his strategy to determine that the decision he'd already made was the right one.

Janice and I also discussed another characteristic of the oldest male with brothers: his ego is tied up in a desire for loyalty. Bob asked Janice not to date other men, even though he was seeing other women, to test her loyalty to him. Would she desert him when the going got rough, or would she love him enough to stick with him? When she learned of this trait, Janice decided just to wait at home for Bob, not pressuring him to give up his dating. She found that he soon abandoned the other girls on his own and shortly thereafter asked her to marry him. Since their marriage he has been a loving and faithful husband.

Oldest males with younger brothers usually marry either last-born females who have older brothers or firstborn females with younger brothers. In both cases the women have experience dealing with men and generally appreciate and admire them (an attitude the oldest male thrives on). The most difficult marriage would result if the oldest brother married the oldest sister with only sisters. Both would have no experience living with the opposite sex; they would also fight for dominance in the family since both are accustomed to leadership roles. This is true to some extent if he chooses to marry a young lady who is the firstborn with younger brothers. There will also be a struggle for control with her, but he will still be attracted to her maternal nature—she replaces his mother.

This portrait of a high-achieving, in-control man, who makes high standards and obedience to the laws of God and man a part of his life, requires a good background, with concerned parents and a stable family life in which to learn proper values. Under adverse circumstances, the very strengths that characterize the oldest brother may be his downfall.

I had a friend in high school whose mother had been married five times. Jack had no stable father; in fact, for years he wasn't sure who his father was. Jack had one brother, a happy-go-lucky boy who was always getting into minor scrapes. Jack married very young and had two children by the time he was twenty. Although he loved his wife, he frequently cheated on her and eventually began to beat her. His life was going nowhere when his daughter died. This was more than Jack could stand, and one day he drove out to the child's grave and killed himself. He had been a tough, hard man, who knew he wasn't treating his family correctly. Even though he had never had a decent male model in his life, he knew that he was falling short of standards. He couldn't live with the guilt and took the only option he could see—suicide.

In summary, the firstborn male with younger brothers will appear on the surface to be a tough man. But underneath he has a strong sense of fairness and morality. He usually won't be able to tolerate disorder or rejections of his authority. But he will appreciate loyalty in his mate and, like other men, will respond positively to a woman who respects him.

The Firstborn Male with Younger Sisters

In sharp contrast to the oldest male with brothers, the oldest male with sisters loves to be around women and feels totally comfortable with them. "What's the use of pursuing wealth or fame," he may ask, "if not to win the love and admiration of women?" Although this man has the firstborn traits of responsibility, conscientiousness, and achievement, his ego won't be satisfied unless his pursuits involve women; he must work with them, protect them, provide for them, or win them. From an early age his parents have told him, "Take care of your sister. Be nice to her." And he has taken their admonitions seriously. He has learned to treat women well.

These men often arrange their lives around the wishes and desires of their women. Tom worked diligently in high school and college so that his grades would be high enough to land him a good job in industrial management. His high-school sweetheart longed for status and social position, and he meant for her to have it. He eventually married her and became a very successful manager, so successful, in fact, that he was never at home. Eventually his family life suffered, and his wife asked for a separation. Tom was crushed; he was about to lose the very thing that gave his life meaning. So he found a less-demanding position that enabled him to spend plenty of time with his wife and children. The marriage revived, and Tom felt at peace once more.

The one thing that would present real ego problems for an oldest male with sisters would be isolation from women. These men would hate a prolonged arctic expedition, a two-month shuttle ride to the moon, or a stint in the army. Even a brief absence from women is painful. A friend of mine recently reflected on his son's visit from out-of-town: "I hope he never comes again without his wife and daughter. He paced around the house like a caged animal. He just didn't know what to do with himself."

In general, women seem to have few complaints about the oldest male with younger sisters. He has many of the strengths and weaknesses associated with the position of firstborn, including a desire for loyalty from his mate. But he knows how to treat women well and, unlike the firstborn male with younger brothers, he is more secure around women. Thus, he won't present as many ego problems as males in other birth order positions.

The Middle Child

The middle child, with both older and younger brothers and sisters, is the hardest of all to describe. He doesn't have the extreme drive of the oldest brother of brothers, but neither does he have the relaxed optimism of youngest males. He possesses characteristics of many family positions and combines them in a way uniquely his own.

The greatest ego problem a middle child may face is the age-old question, "Who am I?" He may have an identity crisis as he sees some of his friends in hot pursuit of wealth or achievement while others just sit back and enjoy life as it comes. He doesn't quite fit in with either extreme, and he has a hard time deciding just what is his role in life.

Because of his flexibility, the middle child is more susceptible than other birth positions to influences such as temperament or peer pressure. I knew a young man during adolescence who grabbed the attention of every girl he met; he was good-looking, out-going, and a football star just waiting for a professional contract. But one trait stood out above all others: he was easygoing, preferring to give in to others rather than risk a fight. He married the head cheerleader and had two beautiful children. But his friendly, easygoing nature got him in trouble. He continued to attract women, and his wife reacted with jealousy. Rather than take hold of the situation, he let her berate and belittle him both in public and in private until their marriage dissolved. He quickly remarried another girl, not because he was anxious to have another wife, but because the girl kept pushing him, and it was easier to give in than to stand up to her.

This is an example of middle-born flexibility carried to an extreme. More often, the middle-born male fluctuates between two desires: to be a leader, just as he led his younger sibling, and to be a follower, just as he followed the lead of his older sibling. Much of the middle-born man's adjustment depends on how well he integrates these two contrasting desires. If he handles the balancing act well, he will come across as flexible and adaptable. If he handles it poorly, he will appear inconsistent and unpredictable.

James Logan personified the unpredictable side of the middle-born's nature. Handsome, intelligent, and well educated, he seemed an excellent prospect for any woman. And he wanted to get married. But all of his relationships with women seemed to follow the same unfulfilling route.

I happened to counsel one of the young women he broke up with. She was a secretary in the office where James worked. She had recently broken off a three-year relationship with a man she wanted to marry. She was still suffering from that when she took the job that brought her into contact with James. He seemed interested in her. She responded eagerly to his overtures, and the first thing everyone knew, they were heavily involved. The romance seemed headed toward deeper things. But then something happened. Within a matter of weeks, this young lady was in a state of severe emotional depression. She was devastated to the point that she couldn't go to work. Her self-esteem was crushed. It was then that she came to my office.

I had known James for some time. He didn't seem like the heartbreaking type. He had high standards and a sensitive conscience. But between her sobs, the story came out. It was one of inconsistency and unpredictability.

"I don't know why he did the things he did," she said, obviously confused and hurt. "He seemed drawn to me; but when we got close, he would pull away. I've seen this in men before, but he carried it to an extreme. Right now, I'm just so confused that I can't even think."

"What sort of things did he do that confused you?" I asked.

"Nothing I did worked well for long. He said I didn't talk enough—that I didn't reveal enough of myself to him. Then when I did reveal myself to him, he ran scared. He also picked at me, criticized me. Then when I got my feelings hurt, he would feel guilty and start crying. He couldn't make up his mind about how much initiative he wanted me to take. He would accuse me of being passive. Then when I became more aggressive, he would put me down. Right now he's got me where I don't know if I'm coming or going."

This is the sort of behavior that makes middle-borns hard to understand. Sometimes they come across as very adaptable. I knew one who seemed the master of every situation. He could fit in well at work in situations that required subordination as well as in those that involved leadership. At home he found just the right balance between authority and cooperation.

But the middle-born who has not found the balance between his divergent drives and traits can drive his spouse to distraction. He alternates between extremes. He moves in one direction and then, when you've adjusted to that, he heads the other way. Relating to such a person can be a real challenge. It requires a person who is flexible and sure of her own identity, a person who can handle a variety of ego problems.

The Last-born Male

Parents who awaited the birth of their first child with eagerness and more than a little tension are relaxed and confident by the time the last child comes along. As one mother put it, "The day my first child was born, my whole world changed. It was the climax of nine months of waiting, preparing, and hoping. But when my last child was born, it just seemed that I took a day off from my regular routine, went to the hospital to have the baby, and then returned the next day to life-as-usual." Such tranquil reactions on the part of parents are reflected in the relaxed attitude of the last-born child. He doesn't seem to have the anxieties and insecurities of the firstborn.

The baby of the family has another child (or children) between himself and his parents, thus reducing the impact that the parents might have on him. He grows up around his brothers and sisters (usually their friends, too) so he becomes very comfortable in social situations. The typical day for a firstborn child might center around interactions with his mother, whereas the last-born child generally follows a group of older children around, learning the give and take of interpersonal relations.

"Jeffrey spends more time with his older sister and brother than he does with me," remarked one mother. "This wasn't the way it was for our firstborn."

Thus, the youngest child grows up in a world of children, whereas the oldest grows up in a world of adults. As a result, a little bit of the "child" stays inside the youngest. He will be more spontaneous than the first, with fewer anxieties and worries. Other people are more important to him, but he won't be as attached to them as the firstborn (who was so attached to his parents).

The youngest child emerges as cheerful and optimistic, a natural comedian and entertainer. (After all, haven't his brothers and sisters been laughing at his every antic for as long as he can remember?) He is not as bound by moral laws and standards as is the first child, and he enjoys great popularity among school and neighborhood friends.

It would be hard to find a more cheerful, optimistic teen-ager than David in the Bible, the youngest of eight brothers. A whole army of Israelites cowered in fear of the giant Goliath, but David confidently declared that he would fight the giant himself. He knew that God would take care of him, no matter how impossible and dangerous the situation looked from a human standpoint. He had a childlike faith that God could really use.

In later years, David committed two of the greatest moral sins, adultery and murder, even though he was king of Israel at the time, and supposedly a moral and spiritual leader. He felt deeply repentant and begged God's forgiveness; then he bounced back to his former cheerful and optimistic self. If a firstborn had committed adultery and murder, he probably would have carried his grief and guilt to the grave.

The Youngest Male with Older Brothers

Randy's marriage was on the rocks; the trouble had begun when his daughter was born. Suddenly his wife was completely absorbed in the baby, and Randy had to fend for himself. So he started going out with the boys.

And how he loved it. He could really be himself around them.

As the youngest boy in a family of two sons, Randy had grown up mostly around males. He was always popular with the other boys at school and soon discovered that it was a lot more satisfying to be out having a good time with the guys than staying at home studying. He could never quite figure out his older brother's quest for good grades.

Of course, Randy's wife complained about how much he was gone and especially about the money he was spending. "You know we can't afford all these hunting trips, particularly now that I've quit work to stay home with the baby. . . . We've got to make sure we give her everything she needs. In fact, maybe we should set aside some money for her college education."

Randy had always been the youngest in his family, the one to be taken care of. He had even married a woman several years older than he. Now, suddenly, he had been displaced by another baby, his daughter; and somehow he knew things would never be the same again. His wife didn't dote on him as before; instead of noticing how charming and witty he was, she admired the baby's achievements.

So Randy just kept going out with his friends, leaving his wife and daughter at home. "That's what they want anyway," he thought, "just to enjoy each other. I'm no good for anything but a paycheck."

Randy's ego was not tied up in a desire for professional recognition or personal growth. He wasn't measuring his self-worth by how closely he adhered to a set of rules or standards. What he did care about very much was receiving the admiration and even adoration of his wife. He longed to be her genius, her knight in shining armor, her hero. And it was not until she began focusing her attention more on Randy and less on the baby that their shaky marriage was strengthened.

Randy typifies the youngest boy with an older brother. These men find male friends very important, probably because they spent so much time with their brothers during childhood. Women find them charming, chivalrous, and very much fun to be around. Everything goes well in a relationship with a youngest brother as long as everyone, especially his wife or girlfriend, sees him as someone very special—someone to be admired and even catered to.

The youngest male in a family of boys has his problems, though. He loves to argue. One father I know looks forward to visits from his youngest son with a mixture of pleasure, anxiety, and amusement. "Well, I wonder how long it will take him to get into an argument with me, get his feelings hurt, and storm out of here in a huff?" he says. It often goes just as the father predicts; but the youngest son is so good-natured that he's usually forgotten the whole incident in just a few days.

Youngest sons also like to live above their means. They will sometimes drive their parents or spouse to distraction by buying new clothes, new cars, a new stereo, even when they are in financial difficulty. They also have a hard time accepting responsibility.

Ken was the baby of the family, with only one older brother. While his brother Jerry had always shouldered a lot of responsibility in the family and had excelled in school, Ken had gotten one message from his parents: "Don't worry about it. You're still young. We don't expect you to keep up with Jerry." So Ken didn't worry. In fact, he was still living at home with his parents supporting him when he was thirty. He had lots of girlfriends, but never felt like taking on the responsibilities of marriage or a family. He was a joy to be around; he had a great sense of humor and was very charming. But he never made enough money to support himself, even though he was a college graduate. Of course, Ken's experience was more extreme than that of most youngest males with older brothers, but a somewhat irresponsible attitude is typical of men with this birth order position.

Youngest Brother of Sisters

When a baby boy is born into a family of girls, and especially when he is the last child, you can imagine what happens. Mom and all the sisters vie with each other to get an opportunity to mother him. He is their pride and joy, and they feel privileged just to wait on him.

When the youngest brother of sisters grows up, he continues to evoke these maternal instincts in women. They love to work for him, both at home and in an office setting. They run his errands, clean up his mess, cook his meals, and ask nothing in return except the pleasure of his company.

Some friends of mine have a last-born son who has lived out this scenario. He had one steady girlfriend in his teens, and after that they never saw him with the same girl twice. Every time he brought a girl home for dinner, it was someone they had never met before. His best friend was a married woman he worked with.

The Child Is Father of the Man

Once he invited his parents to his apartment for dinner, and to their amazement he served them an elaborately prepared meal. When they began asking him about the various dishes, they discovered that several different women had helped him prepare the food. One of them had stayed for dinner and to help clean up afterwards. She even accompanied the son and his parents to their car to tell them goodnight. They never had a moment's privacy with their son.

One day the son announced that he was getting married. It took the parents by surprise, to say the least, because they had no idea which of his many girlfriends he had chosen to be his wife. They guessed several names before they finally hit on the right one.

Fortunately, once the son got married, he settled down to one woman and now they have a happy life together. But he still has a number of female employees at work who like nothing better than to take care of his every need.

It might seem as though the youngest son would have few if any ego problems, especially with so many women doting on him, but there are several areas that give him problems. Perhaps the biggest ego threat is the birth of a child, particularly a son. Like the youngest male with older brothers, this man has always been the baby in the family, the precious darling who delighted everyone. Suddenly he is replaced, and he doesn't like the fact that all of his wife's attention is going to another person. But this feeling can also crop up when visitors come to the home and take attention away from him. This man is the crown prince of his home, and he doesn't want anyone else to be the center of attention there.

Arrogance is another ego problem for the last-born male with sisters. He has always been regarded as someone special, and he expects this deferential treatment from everyone. He usually gets it from women; but men often resent the way the youngest brother lets women wait on him and so find it hard to get along with him, much less treat him with deference.

The Only Child

Years ago, when families were larger and life was a lot less complicated, an only child was a rare bird. But today, with readily available birth control, with more and more mothers returning to work, and with the increasing costs of education and rearing children, we see one- and two-child families as more or less the norm. A lot of parents today are choosing to have only one child, whereas in years past having only one child usually resulted from the death of one parent, divorce, or some other family misfortune. So the traits that show up in today's only child might be somewhat different from those we've seen in the past.

Of course, the main characteristic of an only child is his lack of siblings. He has grown up as a child in the presence of two adults. They have usually focused all their love, concern, and support on this young child, expecting him to act maturely on one hand and enjoying keeping him a baby on the other.

Because there are no brothers or sisters to dilute their effectiveness, parents of an only child have an exceptionally strong impact on him. If the parents provide healthy doses of love and discipline, the only child may grow up to be extremely well adjusted. Consider, for example, James Dobson. Here is a man who truly likes himself and is therefore able to relate well to scores of different people. Although he is intelligent, well-educated and very talented in many areas, the characteristic that seems to stand out in most peoples' minds is his relaxed, easy manner. I was talking with an accountant several weeks ago and Jim Dobson's name came up. "Boy, he sure seems at ease with himself," the accountant told me. "I wonder how he can be so comfortable in front of thousands of people?"

It is obvious from reading Dr. Dobson's books and listening to his seminars that he had a loving and beautiful relationship with each of his parents. They both gave him their very best, and now he will always carry with him a legacy of their love and support.

Unfortunately not every only child is so lucky. If he grows up in an unhappy or unstable home environment, the only child has a lot of handicaps to overcome.

A friend of mine named Bill had a loving but overprotective mother and an alcoholic father. When Bill was only five years old, his father left home and never returned. At first he sent irregular support payments for Bill, but soon even these stopped. Bill's mom raised him as best she could, but she had little time to spend with him between working, doing the housework, and cooking. So Bill withdrew into himself and became a hostile young man. He got into fights in the neighborhood; he dropped out of school several times.

When Bill married, he quickly became a problem to his wife. If she did something that upset him he would give her the silent treatment for weeks on end. She would beg his forgiveness for whatever she had done, but nothing would cure his moodiness except time.

Of course, most only children fall somewhere between these two extremes. In general, they have some difficulty adjusting to marriage because they have never experienced a full-time, intimate peer relationship. Indeed, a male only child will often look for a mother-figure in his wife. And his most severe ego threat would be the loss of his parents or their rejection of him.

Birth Order Conflicts in a Marriage

Since birth position can play such a strong role in shaping a child's personality, ego, and outlook on life, it can also create problems for people who have made less-than-ideal birth position matches in marriage. If, for example, an oldest male with brothers marries an oldest female with sisters, they can have real problems adjusting to each other. Both are accustomed to leadership roles in the family, and both will find it very difficult to submit to someone else's authority. Their first year or two together may be a battleground in which they determine who will "rule." Also, neither one has grown up with a sibling of the opposite sex. The husband has grown up with no one but boys, the wife with no one but girls. So they will be struggling to adjust to a member of the opposite sex at the same time they are waging war over dominance. A couple in which an oldest male with younger sisters marries a youngest female with older brothers would have fewer of these problems.

I counseled a couple recently who demonstrate this principle. Jacque was the youngest in his family. He had a happy-go-lucky attitude toward life. He owned his own company and thoroughly enjoyed his work, especially his interactions with clients and employees.

The Child Is Father of the Man

Rose was the oldest of four children, and she had an entirely different outlook. She liked everything to be done in an orderly and well-organized fashion. If she said dinner would be ready at 6:00 P.M., it was on the table at 6:00 on the dot—not 5:59 or 6:01. When Jacque said he would be home at 6:00, he really meant that he'd try to make it between 5:30 and 7:00.

When they came in for counseling, Rose complained about Jacque's irresponsible attitude toward life. "I never know what to expect from him. He can't give me a definite answer about anything. I can't make plans because he comes home at a different time every night."

Jacque had his own set of grievances. "Rose gives me the third-degree every night. She wants to know where I've been, what I've been doing, how long it all took. I feel like a kid being sent to the principal's office."

Jacque and Rose really loved each other, but their orientations toward life were miles apart. Happiness for Jacque meant freedom to go where he wanted to, freedom to stay as long as he cared to, without having to account for his time. Rose, on the other hand, could feel secure only when every detail of life was "nailed down." Once they truly understood the actual differences in their outlooks, each stopped feeling as though the other was sabotaging his happiness, and they began making small adjustments for each other. Jacque, out of a respect for Rose's need for security, began to call home and let her know when he was about to leave work. And Rose, appreciating Jacque's need for independence, stopped grilling him on the day's events.

SIX

Is That All Men Think About?

As I talked with various women and men, I discovered that sex was looked upon as a (sometimes *the*) central part of the male ego. Women were especially likely to make that observation. Men didn't always see the connection between their sexual behavior and their egos, at least without a little direct questioning.

But if the men hadn't been thinking about the connection between ego and sex, their women had certainly made up for that deficit. Many women had made some shrewd observations about how men connect their egos with their sexual behavior.

One of the most common observations we heard was that men are extremely sensitive to any hint of sexual rejection from their wives. Many women even believe that their husbands' identities as men are wrapped up in their wives' response to their sexual initiatives. "Men," one woman told me, "let their successes or failures at sex color their whole outlook on life. A man may be highly successful at work and have many friends, but if he senses that his wife is uninterested in him sexually—if she responds to his sexual advances with coolness, boredom, or disdain—he will feel like a failure as a man."

And some men do not easily forget sexual slights

from their wives. A couple came to me for counseling several months ago because they were having marital problems. The man was in the throes of a mid-life crisis; he would retreat to his room every evening to be alone and especially to avoid his wife. She longed for his companionship and for a return to a satisfying sexual relationship, but he held back. Finally the reason for the husband's behavior came out: twenty years earlier his wife had been unresponsive to his sexual needs. He had suppressed this hurt for many years but now he felt it in full force. The fact that she afterward became readily available to him made little difference. She had at one period rejected his advances, and he still felt the pain intensely.

Many times during a crisis in their lives, men will place even greater emphasis upon their wives' sexual response. The men will be more sensitive to rejection and more likely to define their self-worth according to their sexual behavior. During these times a woman has great power either to help or hurt her man.

Several years ago a friend of mine named Dave experienced a deep depression. At first he became bored with his job and restless because he wasn't getting promoted as fast as he had hoped. He felt isolated from his parents and childhood friends who lived far away. He couldn't find any hobbies that interested him. Finally Dave's life totally lost its zest. He could barely get up enough motivation to dress and shave in the morning. He spent most of the day staring out his window at work, and during the evening at home he sometimes would sit in a darkened room and just think about how meaningless his life was.

Dave's wife became almost frantic in her quest to help

Dave. She would sympathize with his plight, spending long hours listening to Dave recount again and again his tale of woe. She gave him support, love, and understanding. That helped temporarily but soon Dave would be staring out the window again. She got angry with him and told him to stop feeling sorry for himself; but that just caused him to withdraw further into his self-pity. She begged him to seek professional counseling or medical help for his problems; he wouldn't.

Finally she read a book on depression that suggested a new strategy—sexual seduction. That evening she dressed in her most alluring outfit, wore her hair in her husband's favorite style, put on his favorite cologne, and turned the lights down low. Then she invited him to sit with her for a few minutes and talk. She stroked his hair and caressed him, leaving no doubt in his mind of her intention.

Her behavior so shocked and pleased Dave that he momentarily forgot his depression. He thoroughly enjoyed the evening with his wife and then slept soundly for the first night in weeks. But Dave's wife's goal was to help his depression, not just to have an exciting evening together. Fortunately her seduction and later behavior, letting Dave know in subtle ways that she found him very appealing sexually, had the desired effect. While he still experienced periods of depression, through all the pain his ego remained intact. He knew that he was important and exciting to his wife, no matter how low he felt at the time. This knowledge kept him going when his feelings and emotions told him to give up and quit trying. Eventually Dave came out of his depression completely, but he still recalls the experience vividly: "It was really rough to go through. At times I felt no hope and no worth in myself. But it was also a time of fantastic sexual fulfillment in our marriage. I wouldn't have made it without my wife's encouragement."

Several women I interviewed said that their husbands made sexual demands on them at very inopportune times. Some thought that this was a way that their men reassured themselves about their own importance to their wives.

One woman named Eileen had some very strong feelings on this topic: "During the first four or five years we were married, my husband had this uncanny knack of knowing just when I was under a lot of pressure. He would watch me scurry around our apartment, trying to get my work done so that I wouldn't be late for an appointment. He'd gaze at me while I dressed and fixed my hair; and then, just at I was about to rush out the door, he'd come up behind me, put his arms around me, and tell me he wanted to make love. I'd always heard that you shouldn't reject you husband sexually, so I'd go along with him. But all I could think about was how late I'd be."

Eileen's husband (and probably countless other men) frequently sought sexual attention from his wife at very inconvenient times. Doubtless part of the reason was the nature of his male sexual drive. Men become sexually aroused through visual stimulation, so when Eileen's husband saw her getting dressed, he found that scene very exciting. His sexual drive was activated, and it cried out for release.

But perhaps Eileen's husband had deeper, less obvious psychological reasons for his actions. He saw his wife busily preparing for activities with *someone else*, and his insecurity and jealousy might have been aroused.

He didn't feel comfortable saying, "I wish you were staying here with me. Aren't I more important than that appointment?" So he used lovemaking as a test of his importance to Eileen. In essence, he asked her, "Am I important enough for you to postpone your appointment? Are you willing to be late just to please me?" And when she complied with his wishes, she told him, "Yes, you mean more to me than those people who are waiting. Our marriage relationship is the most meaningful thing in my life." As Eileen continually reassured her husband, eventually these incidents of lovemaking at inconvenient times dropped out. Her husband learned to admire her as she got dressed, but to postpone sexual fulfillment until a more appropriate time.

Another area where women say the male ego shows up quite a bit involves the question, "Who initiates sex?" Here women feel caught in a dilemma. "If I don't initiate sex at all, he feels that I'm not interested," one woman observed, "but if I initiate it very much, he feels threatened by my aggressiveness."

There's probably a lot of truth in this observation. Most men seem to want their women to initiate sex just enough to show that they are interested, but not so much as to take away from the man his role as initiator.

Gary and Susan faced a problem of this kind. Gary, an easygoing fellow, was quite a bit older than his new bride, Susan. He already had considerable sexual experience while Susan, an extremely outgoing and upbeat girl, was sexually naive. When they married and Gary introduced Susan to the joys of sex, she became so thrilled with this new experience that she wanted to make love all the time. She would frequently call Gary at work and ask him to "come home early, honey." And when they were at home together, she was always making sexual advances, or so it seemed to Gary. Gary, meanwhile, had a very demanding job and just didn't have the time or energy to fulfill all Susan's desires. And as she kept demanding frequent sex, Gary reacted by spending more time at work and becoming less interested in lovemaking. He slowly withdrew from Susan, both physically and emotionally, eventually taking no interest in anything that she initiated—projects, vacation plans, or whatever.

Couples differ in the extent to which they prefer the husband or the wife to initiate sex. Some men prefer their wives to be at least as initiatory as they are; others want always to initiate themselves. If the wife's sexual initiatives exceed the husband's tolerance level, he may react by becoming impotent or withdrawing. This is what happened to Gary. But not every man reacts as Gary did. Other men may withdraw for the opposite reason—their wives don't show enough sexual interest or initiative.

I once counseled Sally, a woman who carried a rather unusual burden—she had to initiate all the sex in her marriage. Her husband, Frank, was a very successful businessman. He was well respected by his associates and had lots of friends in the community. They had two lovely daughters and, to the casual observer, what seemed to be an almost ideal marriage. But Frank, even though he had every reason to feel sure of himself, had a deep fear of being rejected. He loved Sally and had a strong sexual attraction to her, but he refused to make sexual advances. Sally tried to initiate lovemaking on a regular basis; and if she did, she and Frank got along beautifully. But if Sally got busy or preoccupied and forgot to approach Frank, he would become sullen and withdrawn, opening up only to lash out at the girls or Sally herself. This burden eventually became too much for Sally, and she had to seek counseling to ease her mounting feelings of resentment and guilt.

Ego Differences and Sexual Styles

It's probably fair to say that men relate sexually to women in part according to the way they perceive woman's sexual nature. In the last century, for example, it was commonly believed that women had no sexual drive, that they didn't really enjoy sex and engaged in it only for their men's pleasure. Today, a man would have to be culturally isolated to be unaware of all the challenges to the Victorian interpretation.

In fact, some men are probably under the opposite delusion—that women are multiorgasmic creatures capable of such heights of sexual experience that no single man can satisfy them. That is probably an exaggeration, but men do seem more aware today of women's sexual response than they did several decades ago.

Despite this increase in knowledge, men still differ quite a bit in how they typically relate to their wives sexually. In part, men establish a sexual relationship with their women as a result of personality factors. But other influences, such as values, beliefs and knowledge about sex, and the quality of the marital relationship also play a role.

While it's difficult to pinpoint all possible types of sexual style among men, several patterns seem to show up. One type, the quick draw, is the target of much resentment among women. This is the man who wants one thing out of sex—his own climax. He generally dispenses with foreplay and doesn't show much concern for his wife's sexual response. To him sex is mainly a tension release.

Not surprisingly, these men show a similar insensitivity in other areas of their lives. They are often driven men at work, putting in long hours. They have a no-nonsense approach to life, appear hard-boiled and usually scoff at what appears to them as impractical—literature, philosophy, and art, for example. They are often impatient in general, as well as in bed.

The second type of sexual style is that of the artist. He sees sex as a skill, and he puts much of himself into it. He is often highly motivated to have his mate enjoy sex as well as to enjoy it himself. He will spend much time in foreplay. And he has learned one secret of helping a woman enjoy sex to the maximum: he is sensitive to her particular needs before and during the act. He behaves with intimate, loving care. Not surprisingly, his woman is very sexually satisfied.

Oftentimes these men show the same artistry and skill in other areas of their lives. At work they are efficient and effective, without putting in the long hours the quick draw prefers. The artist substitutes quality for quantity. His ego is based upon a job well done.

The third type of sexual style is that of the dominator. This man sees sex as an opportunity to express his most compelling needs—to control and dominate. He is often the man who insists on sex at the most inopportune moments as a way of verifying his own control. However, many men do this for other reasons, such as the need for reassurance, or jealousy.

If he is concerned with his mate's satisfaction, he will

often come on like the artist (if his own control is first established). But if he is insensitive to his spouse, he looks more like the quick draw.

Dominators are usually men who have to initate sex themselves if they are to enjoy it. They will not be receptive to their wife's initiation. Frequently they also can't take suggestions in other matters from their wives (or from others) and thus tend to rise and fall only on their own knowledge and skill level.

The fourth type of sexual style belongs to the conqueror. This man has a need to conquer, to meet and master a challenge, as part of his sexual drive. He is the man who, when single, sees women as potential notches on his gun handle. As a husband, he has a lot of trouble remaining faithful. Other women look too tempting. The enjoyment is in the pursuit. Once he has conquered, he loses interest.

As sexual partners, these men typically have an interest span that's too short for them to be really good lovers. Sex is too routine if it's not accompanied by the thrill of a challenge or a chase. Wise spouses quickly learn to keep these men off-balance and guessing, usually by pulling back emotionally and playing hard-to-get.

These men generally do well in business and industry, at least for a while, because they are willing to take risks. Many times, though, they get in trouble by risking too much or by continuing to pursue a project long after it becomes obvious that it's a dead-end street.

How Men and Women View Sex

When women take what they know about themselves and try to apply it to the men in their lives, they frequently run into trouble. This is never more apparent than in the area of sexuality.

In general, men view sex as a very strong need in their lives, but they do not necessarily tie their sexual needs in with their other needs for companionship, security, and emotional support. Men have an uncanny way of parceling themselves out with little or no conflict unless, of course, they are committed to strong religious or ethical principles. And this ability of men to break up their lives into different compartments can devastate women, who approach life from the opposite perspective. Many of my clients have faced the dilemma of this "double standard," but one in particular stands out in my mind.

Bonnie got a job as a legal secretary right after she graduated from high school. She worked several years for a small law firm and then had the opportunity to work as the private secretary for a young lawyer who was just setting up his practice. The challenge intrigued Bonnie, so she accepted the new position with great enthusiasm. The young lawyer was very intelligent and good-looking; he seemed to have everything going for him, including a wife who was already an established member of another law firm.

The lawyer was extra-nice to Bonnie, and she loved the attention. He discussed cases with her and took her out to lunch at least once a week. Before Bonnie realized what had happened, she had fallen in love with her boss. She was determined, however, that he would never know her true feelings for him.

Unfortunately the lawyer was having marital problems and turned to Bonnie for comfort and support. She was thrilled. Her self-esteem soared. And when the lawyer asked her to accompany him on an overnight business trip, she just couldn't turn him down. She had visions of saving him from an unhappy marriage while at the same time being rescued herself from a life of loneliness.

Bonnie soon realized that her dream world was becoming a nightmare. Her affair with the lawyer was going nowhere. He had no intention of leaving his wife, yet he continued to profess great love for Bonnie. His attention, which had once been a source of great self-esteem for Bonnie, now made her feel cheap. She hated herself for becoming involved with a married man, but she saw no way out.

Finally Bonnie moved to another state, more out of a sense of desperation than from a real desire to start over. She had to find some way to regain her shattered self-respect. But the lawyer found out where she had gone and began calling her every evening, still declaring his love and loyalty to her. He came to see her about once a month, keeping her life filled with guilt, hurt, and confusion.

When Bonnie came to see me, all she could think of was escaping her dependence on this lawyer. She wanted to be free of him so she could find a new life of her own. She had looked to him to meet all of her needs, and he had failed miserably. While she had given herself totally to him, he had given himself only emotionally and sexually. He had never considered leaving his wife, who gave him security, respectability, and added social standing because of her professional position. He had parceled out his "favors" to two women, leaving them both hurt and unfulfilled, while he felt almost comfortable with the arrangement.

Sexual Problems that Affect a Man's Ego

The tie between a man's sexuality and his ego becomes very apparent when he has a problem with sexual dysfunction. The cause of the dysfunction may be totally beyond the man's control, but still he sees it as a reflection on his overall worth and value as a person.

One problem that has come to my attention quite recently is the dramatic decrease in sexual drive that results from taking certain kinds of medication. Men must take medication to prevent high blood pressure or heart attack, for example, but often their general health improves at the expense of their sex lives . . . and at the expense of their egos, too.

Kirk and Jenny had been married over thirty years when Kirk had his first heart attack. Prior to the attack, Kirk had been a very successful salesman, throwing a lot of his time and energy into work. He and Jenny had a very active sex life, too, as well as a happy and fulfilling marriage. But the heart attack changed all that. Kirk was hospitalized for about two weeks and then had to recuperate at home for several more months. During this time, he noticed that he had almost no desire for sexual relations with his wife, but he attributed that to his fear of another heart attack. When the doctor gave him the go-ahead on all his regular activities except work, he expected to resume his sex life just as before. But when he and his wife attempted intercourse, he found himself almost impotent. He made a quick call to the doctor and discovered some shattering news. "You'll just have to live with this problem for a while," the doctor told him dispassionately. "Our first concern is to get you well."

At this point, Kirk didn't care if he got well or not. What good would it do him to live a long life if he couldn't work to support his family and couldn't even have sex with his wife? He became depressed and withdrawn, turning to alcohol to comfort him and block out the nagging thoughts about his inadequacy as a man.

Jenny, too, became despondent as she saw such a dramatic change in Kirk. She could easily have lived without frequent sex, but it hurt her deeply to see Kirk's ego so shattered by his impotence. She told me, "I don't know what to say or do. If I tell Kirk that sex really isn't that important to me, he feels as if all the times we were together before the attack weren't that meaningful to me. But I surely can't say that I miss our active sex life. . . . That would really crush him. I just don't know how to relate to a man whose ego has been so badly damaged."

Of course, not all men who face this problem react as Kirk did. Some, like Steve, make the necessary adjustments in their lives with creativity and confidence, thus building up their egos in the process. (Notice, too, that I met Kirk while he was in the midst of discovering his problem, and I met Steve after he had made a satisfactory adjustment to his. Time can be a great healer, as Kirk will probably discover.)

Steve and his wife had three teen-age children when the doctor found out he had heart disease. He had to take medication similar to Kirk's and soon realized he, too, had problems with low sex drive. At first he felt devastated by his loss of virility, but he quickly learned new ways to "make love" to his wife. He became extremely thoughtful of her, buying her lovely gifts and calling her often when he was out of town. He discovered little ways of showing love and appreciation— stroking her hair or noticing how nice she looked in a new dress. His marriage stayed strong and vital, despite a much-reduced sex life. And his ego, though shaken momentarily, remained firmly intact.

Sometimes a man's sexual problem does not directly involve his performance during intercourse; he may be the epitome of virility and still face the ego-deflating dilemma of infertility.

Several years ago the television series "Barney Miller" dealt with this topic. One of the main characters, a real lady's man name Stanley Wojohowitz, was named as the defendant in a paternity suit. He had had so many girlfriends that he couldn't even remember which one was claiming him as the father of her child. He went to have tests run to determine if he were, in fact, the child's father; but he found out, instead, that he was sterile. He went into shock and then depression. He felt as though he had been castrated even though he was as capable of sexual performance as ever. There was nothing his fellow police officers could say to ease the pain of Wojo's wounded ego.

While the writers of "Barney Miller" used the subject of infertility as a source of humor, for most men this is no laughing matter. It strikes at the heart of their self-concept, often causing serious damage to their self-esteem. As one man told a *Newsweek* reporter, "There is nothing that hits into the very essence of what I am as a man more than this."[1]

Infertility afflicts approximately three-and-one-half million American couples; and in about 40 percent of the cases, the problem lies with the man. But whichever spouse has reproductive difficulties, this problem affects both husband and wife intensely. Not only must a sterile man deal with his own ego-deflation; he must also contend with his wife's frustration, pain, and despair.

After visiting fertility clinics, having scores of tests done, and submitting to surgery if necessary, what can the man do who still finds himself infertile? Probably his best strategy would be to emphasize other areas of his life, especially his work, in order to reestablish his sense of potency. In this way, he can build up his beleaguered ego and gain sufficient peace of mind so that he could help his wife cope with her own disappointments.

This is what Brent did. He and his wife, Wendy, had one child and planned to have at least two more. But Wendy could not get pregnant again. After three years of trying unsuccessfully on their own, Brent and Wendy went to a fertility specialist and spent countless hours and a great deal of money on tests to determine exactly what their problem was. It turned out that both had structural difficulties, so each of them underwent surgical procedures to improve their chances of having a baby. Unfortunately nothing helped, and they had to face the prospects of either raising their child alone or adopting other children. While they were going through the tests and surgeries, both Brent and Wendy became increasingly involved in other areas of interest, subconsciously insulating themselves from further pain over their failure to have children. Brent, a pastor, developed creative and innovative techniques for capturing the attention of his congregation, especially the young people. He also went out of his way to spend extra time with his child, allowing his wife to pursue further education.

Brent and Wendy took an undesirable situation, a situation loaded with the potential for inflicting pain and blame on each other, and made the best of it. They directed their interests and energies into new areas, instead of taking their frustrations out on each other and possibly damaging their marriage.

SEVEN

Here Comes the Judge

Janet and Larry had their most explosive marital arguments over the issue of how Janet related to friends that Larry didn't like. One friend in particular set them against each other. She was Janet's co-worker, and Janet's friend as well, at least until Janet married Larry. The friend, named Helen, didn't approve of Larry, and she told Janet so before they were married. Larry felt the same way about Helen; she was a bad influence on Janet, he thought.

In the months before they married, Helen was an unpleasant topic of conversation for Janet and Larry. But several months after the wedding, her name became anathema.

The problem exploded when Larry found out that Helen had said some negative things about him to Janet and Janet had not defended him.

"How could she sit there and let this woman run down her own husband and not say anything in my defense?" Larry angrily blurted out.

"But Larry, you know that happened during a time when we were having marital problems, and I felt negatively about you and the marriage. I would defend you today, since we're getting along better," Janet replied.

That didn't seem to make it any better for Larry. In

fact, the disagreement reheated whenever Janet bumped into Helen and was nice to her. Larry felt that Janet should not converse socially with Helen at all. Janet feared that Larry was trying to tell her how to conduct her social life.

Their disagreement over Helen uncovered some deep feelings on both parts. As they tossed it back and forth in my office, Janet began to look more and more like a cornered person. The more Larry stated his position, the more threatened and defensive Janet appeared. Larry's irritation increased in proportion to Janet's refusal to adopt his suggestions.

Initially, the whole issue seemed to have been blown out of proportion to its importance. But as they continued to argue, I began to see how their failure to resolve the conflict resulted from some basic differences in the way the two spouses thought about problems and issues.

To Janet, all that mattered was her relationship with Helen. She had been friends with Helen for several years; the two had liked each other for quite a long time, and there was no reason to treat Helen any differently now.

But to Larry, it was "the principle of the thing. If someone runs your spouse down, you cease having anything to do with that person. No one should come between spouses. It's as pure and simple as that."

Janet felt threatened that Larry would go so far as to dictate to her the boundaries of a relationship. Larry was frustrated and angry over Janet's unwillingness to respect this principle that was so clear to him.

Initially I tried to resolve the situation by encouraging Larry to adopt a different principle. "You've chosen to look at this from the standpoint of the law of reciprocity," I said to Larry. "There are other principles that could apply—forgiveness, letting your spouse be herself."

But Larry wouldn't be moved. "Helen is a threat to the marriage. I say that each of us should reject anyone or anything that comes between husband and wife."

Since I'd gotten nowhere with that approach, I tried a different tactic. If I couldn't get either to change their position, I could at least get them to understand each other. Hopefully after understanding the differences and what caused them, they would have more respect and empathy for one another.

I turned to both and explained basically what I wrote three paragraphs ago: Janet was relationship oriented, and Larry was preoccupied with laws, rules, and principles.

That approach seemed to work. They didn't reach a precise agreement about how to treat Helen. But they did learn to understand their differences and to respect each others' positions. This caused the emotion to go out of the argument, and the issue to take a back seat to more important concerns.

Perhaps that's the most important thing that can come out of discussions of male and female differences. We won't make one sex become like the other. But we can understand the strengths and weaknesses that each brings to the relationship. Out of that understanding, we hope, can come respect and appreciation.

The way that men and women think about moral problems and resolve issues that involve values are important determinants of how they get along. And the simple fact is that men and women think differently about issues of morality, especially those that directly involve other people. Morals, standards, and conscience operate differently in the male ego. As we shall see, men both approach and solve moral dilemmas in a way that sounds on the surface better than the way women do. But don't let the surface fool you.

Men and Women and Morality

I'll never forget the first time I had to teach Freud's theory of human behavior to a class of graduate students. Freud was one of the first great psychologists, and many of his observations were groundbreaking. But parts of his theory seem ridiculous to me, and are very difficult to explain, even to a group of intelligent adults.

One of his strangest ideas is that the male conscience is stronger than the female conscience—in other words, that men have a more advanced level of moral thinking than do women. "How could this be true," I always wondered when I considered this theory, "when men are responsible for most of the gross immorality that we see in the world?"

Nevertheless, Freud's theory had to be covered in class, so I plunged in. I hardly got the words out of my mouth when up shot the hand of one of my female students: "This flies in the face of common sense!" she exclaimed. "It's usually males who commit the crimes, males who leave their families, males who start the wars. How could Freud have believed that drivel?" So it seemed to her, to me, and to most of the other students a case where theory clashed with reality.

Nevertheless, I soon discovered that there had to be at least some validity to Freud's theory. I began studying the work of Lawrence Kohlberg, a Harvard psychologist, who devised a scale of moral development and also a test that places people on a continuum of moral development. Those scoring at the low end of the continuum have the least developed sense of morality (they do what is right only to avoid punishment or to gain some reward). Those scoring at the upper end have the highest level of morality (they have internalized rules and principles and act on the basis of a finely-tuned conscience). Those scoring in the middle of the continuum tend to adopt the rules and principles of people around them (they "follow the crowd").

When I got to Kohlberg's work on sex differences, my interest really picked up. To my surprise and even amazement, Kohlberg also found that males tend to have a more advanced level of moral development than do females. Among the people that Kohlberg tested, males as a group scored higher on the continuum than did the females.

At first glance, this sounds incredible. Think about the most heinous type of crime possible—mass murder. Do women ever commit mass murder? Hardly. As I wrote this chapter one of the strangest cases I've seen had just been wrapped up.

Recently I read a newspaper article on the Christine Fallings murder trial. Miss Fallings had been present, usually as a babysitter, at the deaths of five infants or small children. Incredibly, though, there was no evidence that any of these children were murdered. All their deaths had been attributed to natural causes. The reporter interviewed a physician who made the point that there was one chance in a million that five children would have died from natural causes while in the care of one person. But did he suspect murder? Not necessarily, because the occurrence of female mass murderers is about one-in-a-million, too.

I can think of at least five male mass murderers without even trying; there seem to be one or two every year. But here was a female mass murderer, something I had never heard of. How could Freud and Kohlberg have possibly concluded that males have stronger consciences?

Despite the research Kohlberg had done, the idea that women engage in less sophisticated moral thinking than men seemed ludicrous until another Harvard psychologist—Carol Gilligan—published a fascinating book entitled *In a Different Voice*.[1] Dr. Gilligan has devoted her career to studying male and female moral thinking. Once again, she found that males score at higher levels on moral development scales than do females. But finally she shed some light on the reason why this is so. Dr. Gilligan believes that the definition of moral development that psychologists have come up with favors the male style of thinking and overlooks the nature of female moral development.

For example, Kohlberg's test of moral growth sees higher morality as increasingly involved with principles, rules, and laws, rather than with people and human relationships. And according to Gilligan, this one-sided definition favors men over women. As they mature, males become more abstract and impersonal; they focus on gaining independence and become involved in the search for truth through rules, laws, and principles. Relationships take a back seat to the quest for achievement and advancement. Take, for example, the cases of Martin Luther and Saint Jerome. These were two spiritual giants who greatly advanced humankind's grasp of God's mercy. Yet both were more involved with pure laws and principles and not as involved with people, including their own families. Both men had few intimate relationships.

We also see examples today of men whose egos are more dependent on rules and principles than they are on people. I met a man several years ago who, because of family financial problems, had to leave home in his early teens to find a job. He worked his way through high school and several years of college. He married in his late twenties and set out to establish himself as a successful businessman. He worked for a large company for a while, but always yearned to own his own business. When he heard about a small dry cleaning firm that was for sale, he scraped together all the money he could get his hands on and bought it. He wasn't satisfied to have a moderately successful business, though. He had seen how financial problems had hurt his family and disrupted his life at an early age, so he was determined to succeed. He had one goal that ruled his life— providing such a good income for his family that they would never have to worry about money. He worked twelve to fourteen hours a day, seven days a week, coming home only to eat and sleep. His wife begged him to take it easy, especially once the business was flourishing. She planned vacations for the family, only to have him back out at the last minute because he needed to be at work. This man loved his family so much that he was willing to make any sacrifice for them. Yet he hardly had thirty minutes a day to spend with his wife and daughter. He fulfilled his goal in life splendidly, but ended up almost a stranger to the ones he loved. He, like all-too-many other men, had sacrificed a close relationship with his family in pursuit of a goal.

Dr. Gilligan paints an altogether different picture of females. Women, she says, are imbedded in a web of close relationships. Their development centers around a search for people and intimacy rather than for principles, laws, or lofty moral goals.

In a recent psychological study, researchers found that not only do women need and enjoy social interaction, but both sexes profit more from interacting with women than with men. Both male and female college students were tested for their level of anxiety and then were divided into two groups—those with low anxiety and those with high anxiety. Next the two groups of students had to list the conversations they had engaged in during the previous week. The researchers found that the low anxiety group, those who felt secure and comfortable with themselves, had talked predominantly with women the week before. The high anxiety group had had fewer conversations with women. Therefore, the psychologists conducting this study concluded that both men and women are more secure and their anxiety level is lower, if they can talk with women.

I have noticed this phenomenon in my own wife, too, every time we make a long-distance move. For the first week or so Evelyn is engrossed in unpacking and getting settled. But about the second week she starts to get vaguely uneasy and dissatisfied. This discontent increases until she can find other women that she can strike up close relationships with. Once that "sisterhood" is established, she returns to her optimistic self.

Strangely enough, not only do men not seem to need

this kind of close relationship to other men, they generally avoid it. They fear losing their independence by becoming too close to someone else; they are apprehensive about being swallowed up by another person. So they retreat to the safety of rules and regulations. Their relationships are downplayed while principles and impersonal logic are enthroned. Similarly, men are often willing to give up relationships for achievement or advancement.

For women, the opposite is true. Women see danger in separation, competition, or achievement because these things threaten the intimacy that women value so highly. I have known several women who were very intelligent, but kept their school grades or professional accomplishments a secret for fear of jeopardizing friendships with people who hadn't reached their level of achievement. Human relationships are so important and satisfying to women that they are often willing even to give up achievement for them.

These differing tendencies of men and women showed up graphically in one phase of Dr. Gilligan's research. She conducted several studies with the Thematic Apperception Test (TAT), a test that requires an experimenter to show ambiguous pictures to people and then ask them to tell a story about the pictures. What she found was that men's aggressive impulses were aroused by scenes of intimacy. When she showed pictures of men and women in close relationships, the men often told stories that were filled with violence or accidents. When she showed them pictures of individuals in competition or activity, on the other hand, they told more pleasant stories. With women, Dr. Gilligan found the opposite results.

One picture in particular demonstrates this principle quite well. Dr. Gilligan showed both men and women an illustration of a male and female trapeze team. The man was portrayed as the catcher; he had his legs wrapped around the trapeze as he flew through the air. Meanwhile the woman was moving toward him and her hands were almost touching his. When men saw this illustration, they often told hostile or aggressive stories about the woman falling or getting hurt. Women, on the other hand, told positive stories about the man and woman in a very close relationship.

Considering the risks involved in a trapeze act, at first glance one might think that the stories describing accidents would be the more appropriate ones. But when the researchers questioned the women about their lack of dangerous stories, the women explained that their couple had a safety net below them, even though the picture showed only a close-up view of the man and woman, with the safety net out of view. It seems that the women just assumed that with a good relationship, the environment would be nonthreatening. Men, on the other hand, assumed no safety net. The closeness of the man and woman signaled potential danger and made them feel uncomfortable.

Implications

1. *Dependence on one woman.* Because men are so wrapped up in gaining independence and establishing themselves as individuals, they generally tend to isolate themselves. Research has repeatedly shown that men rarely have intimate friendships, certainly nothing like women have. But men still need social contact, love,

and understanding. They focus many or all of their needs on their wives; in other words, they often put all of their emotional eggs in one basket.

Perhaps this is one of the reasons that the male ego is perceived as fragile by women. Men find it hard to become vulnerable enough to open up to another person, and they do so with a certain sense of fear. With their wives, girlfriends, or mothers, they give up some of their independence and power in exchange for emotional support and comfort. Thus they are easily wounded when these especially-trusted women seem to turn on them. Temporarily, at least, men may decide that isolation is preferable to pain. This was the theme of Simon and Garfunkel's song, "I Am a Rock."

2. *A spiritual emphasis on law and faith.* As we have seen, principles take precedence over relationships for men. Dr. Gilligan finds examples of this in the Bible also. In one extremely poignant and dramatic scene, human life, the life of a beloved son, is deemed less important than the principle of obeying God (see Gen. 15—22).

Abraham had been given the promise that he would be the father of nations. He waited for the fulfillment of this promise in the form of his wife, Sarah's, pregnancy; but years went by and there was no child. Finally Sarah and Abraham, frustrated and discouraged by the long delay, took matters into their own hands. Abraham had a child by Sarah's maid. Years later Sarah and Abraham had a child of their own. Anyone who has waited even a year or two for a child knows how thrilling it is finally to hold the longed-for baby. Imagine how ecstatic and awed Abraham and Sarah must have been after waiting for decades! Abraham and Sarah adored Isaac and thanked God for him often. But one night Abraham received a horrifying message from God—he was to sacrifice his own son Isaac, the promised child. How law and love must have battled that night. But in the end, Abraham obeyed God. The highest morality for Abraham was to trust God, to believe so much in the wisdom of this eternal, unseen force, that he could give up his own son. Principle held sway over relationship.

There was a woman in the Bible, too, who made a conscious decision to give up her child (see 1 Kin. 3:16–28). It seemed that there were two women who lived in the same house and who had babies of approximately the same age. One woman accidentally rolled over on her baby during the night and killed him. In her grief and despair at discovering her lifeless child, she stole the other woman's baby, claimed him as her own, and put the dead baby in the other woman's bed. The real mother, upon realizing the cruel trick that had been played on her, appealed to King Solomon for the return of her child. The king brought both women and the child into his court. It was one woman's word against the other. One woman was telling the truth; one was lying out of grief, pain, and desperation.

So Solomon, according to the Bible the wisest man who ever lived, appealed not to principle, but to a mother's love to solve the dilemma. He seized a sword and offered to cut the child in half so that each woman could have part of the baby. The hideous suggestion immediately brought an outcry from the real mother. "Oh, no sir! Give her the child—don't kill him." This mother no longer cared about truth or falsehood; she no longer sought to have justice done. Principle was thrown to the wind in order to save the life of her child.

Both Abraham and this unnamed mother had to make the decision to give up a child. Abraham was called upon to do so out of principle; the mother out of love. (Note, too, that God called upon Abraham, not Sarah, to make the sacrifice of Isaac out of faith and principle.)

Since God made us, He is of course aware of our psychological make-up. He uses this knowledge as He deals differently with men and women in the Bible. When God called Abraham, he was living with his wife Sarah and his nephew Lot in his father's house in Haran. God gave Abraham a very direct command, "Get out of your country, from your kindred and from your father's house, to a land that I will show you" (Gen. 12:1). But in addition to the command, God promised Abraham great blessings, great opportunities to establish his independence and make a significant contribution to mankind, incentives a man would find most attractive: "I will make you a great nation; I will bless you and make your name great; and you shall be a blessing. . . . and in you all the families of the earth shall be blessed" (Gen. 12:2–3).

Abraham, at the age of seventy-five, left home to follow God. He had no idea where God would lead him or how long his travels would last. He stepped out in faith, trusting God and looking forward to rich rewards.

When God chose to call a woman out of her homeland so that she could share a closer walk with Him, He used an entirely different method. An entire book of the Bible is devoted to the dealings of God with a young woman who was not even one of the children of Israel (see Ruth). It seems that there was a famine in the land of Israel, so a man named Elimelech moved with his wife and two sons to Moab. While the family lived in Moab the sons grew up and eventually married Moabite women. Unfortunately all three men died, leaving a widowed mother-in-law and two widowed daughters-in-law to fend for themselves. Apparently during the time of this narrative, a woman without a man, either a husband, brother, or son, was virtually helpless and defenseless, unable to support herself in any form. So these three women were in desperate straits.

The mother-in-law, Naomi, decided to return to her homeland, Israel, where she might find refuge with relatives. She must have had an extremely close and loving relationship with her daughters-in-law because both of them chose to leave their homes and move to Israel with her. Naomi, although she loved them dearly, felt that they would be happier and in more stable circumstances if they remained in Moab, and she begged them to stay. One daughter-in-law finally agreed to stay behind. But the other, Ruth, spoke the classic words, "Entreat me not to leave you, or to turn back from following after you; for wherever you go, I will go; and wherever you lodge, I will lodge; your people shall be my people, and your God, my God" (Ruth 1:16).

Ruth accompanied Naomi back to Bethlehem, her home, and eventually met and married a man named Boaz, "a man of great wealth" (Ruth 2:1). She had left her father and mother, she had departed her homeland, because of a great love and respect for her mother-in-law. But she gained a closer relationship with God and a wealthy and loving husband in the process.

The examples illustrate well the differences between men and women in moral thinking. Men, more detached and objective, think in terms of laws, principles, and goals. Women, more intimate and personal, think in terms of people and relationships.

This means that no matter how moral and advanced a

man may be, he is not likely to be as intimate in relationships as is his wife. His ego does not let him easily reach out toward others, but rather he reacts like a judge—weighing, analyzing, evaluating, and often punishing. That's one of the negative parts of male morality—it can too easily lead to a punitive, impersonal approach to humans.

An interesting illustration of men as judges and punishers and women as forgivers and nurturers showed up in a recent *Newsweek* magazine essay.[2] The author, Elizabeth Mehren, described how she had been the victim of assault and attempted rape by a man who had at one time been a close friend of hers. He had beaten her, pinned her to the floor, and dragged her by the hair. When she told her friends about the ordeal, she was fascinated to discover that their advice to her split along sex lines: almost universally the men cried out for vengeance while the women urged her to forget it ever happened and go on with living. While the men offered to punish the man personally (her brother volunteered to "fly out and kill him," and a TV executive said he would be glad to "surgically remove his masculinity"), the women took her out to eat and ordered expensive champagne, sent her flowers, and slipped her Valium tablets. The men urged, even insisted, that she take legal action, and the women told her, "Don't be a martyr for principle."

Of course, both the impersonal, punitive approach and the personal, humane approach to morality are needed. But the "male" approach to justice, being more abstract, results in a more detached pattern of human relationships and a larger set of barriers to intimacy.

EIGHT

Handling Men with Ego Problems

The male ego is a heated topic for many women. We learned that as we interviewed a variety of wives, girlfriends, and mothers. Eyes often flashed and voices elevated in pitch as women described their men's ego problems.

At first we asked women detailed questions about the male ego. But we soon found that a single open-ended question such as, "What can you tell me about the male ego?" would send women off into a prolonged discussion (sometimes a tirade). Much emotion is connected with this topic.

Many specific questions arose from those interviews. When asked what sort of ego problems their husbands or boyfriends had, many women in turn questioned us about ways to deal with their men's ego-related problems. These questions ranged from one husband beating his wife when he had problems at work to another wanting his breakfast in bed, from a fiancé extending the engagement for six years to a son who didn't want to be seen in public with his mother.

In this chapter, I will suggest some ways women can deal with the male ego. I've taken the most common questions women asked and grouped them into several topic areas.

Understanding the Male Ego

Before I answer specific questions about male ego problems, I'd like to discuss some general ways that you can change another person. Bringing about change in other people is, of course, what psychotherapy and counseling are all about. Psychologists have amassed a wealth of techniques for facilitating change in others. But those techniques can be placed in a small number of categories—three to be exact.

The most common way that people attempt to change something in another person is to *oppose it*. If, for example, your child wants to eat snacks all day (and then won't eat his vegetables at supper), you limit the amount of snacks he eats; you explain to him how important it is to eat properly; and you encourage, wheedle, or coerce him to eat a balanced meal at suppertime. If necessary you offer him a reward (dessert) if he finishes all his vegetables. In short, you oppose his desire to eat snacks improperly.

This sounds like a negative technique, but it's not necessarily such. You can oppose a behavior or an attitude by encouraging the person in another direction. For example, most of us, when we hear that a friend is depressed, will say something such as "Cheer up. It could be a lot worse. You've got a lot to be happy about." We are opposing his depression and encouraging him to change it.

You could influence this depressed person to change in other ways that would oppose his or her depression. You could give a reward for not being depressed. In other words, you could give your attention when he or she acts cheerful and ignore him or her when he or she acts depressed. If he or she begins telling you how bad everything looks, how things aren't getting any better, how he or she can't take it anymore, you could glance around the room looking bored, maybe even yawn. (This should be done subtly, of course; you are not out to hurt feelings but to help a friend overcome depression.)

If, on the other hand, he or she says something positive like, "I saw an interesting article in the paper last night," you should give your full attention, look him or her directly in the eye, and perhaps lean forward in your chair to show how interested you are in what he or she has to say.

There are still other response techniques to behavior such as depression. You could demand that your depressed friend cheer up, giving lectures and generally nagging him or her into cheerfulness (if such a thing is possible). Finally, you could suggest that he or she might live a better life if he or she didn't give in to the depression. All these are ways to change a person by opposing his or her present behavior. They generally work quite well if you are persistent, but kind. Sometimes, though, these methods don't seem to budge the person we're trying to change. We have to go to a completely different strategy.

The second way you can bring about change in another person is to *accommodate them*. That is, you can take the behavior they're displaying and ask them to do more of it, or do more yourself.

The depressed person, for example, won't respond when you oppose his or her unhappiness. So you go along with it. When he or she says that life is not worth living, you agree: "You're right. I don't know if it's worth it either. I feel the same way you do."

This sounds bizarre, but it's often the only thing that

will work in the case of a person who won't respond to the oppositional approach. In fact, I've observed quite a few marriages where the husband was chronically depressed and the wife responded by trying hard to cheer him up, always being cheerful herself, rushing to wait on him when he came crashing down, and in general doing all in her power to oppose his depression. The husband never changed. So the wife learned to agree with his depression, to tell him it was worse than even he thought, and to become somewhat depressed herself. The husband responded by losing his depression.

This is not the sort of strategy you'd want to try first. But as a last resort it often works when nothing else will.

I once counseled a couple in which the husband was schizophrenic. He was convinced that everyone was staring at him because of his skin condition. (His skin was actually fine.) He would tell his wife in detail about how people had stared at him all day, and she would argue with him. On and on this went until one day, in desperation, she tried a new tactic.

Instead of arguing with him, she agreed with him. "You're right," she said, "people are staring at you. Cars are stopping and people are looking and pointing." In an amazingly short space of time, he quit reporting that people were staring at him.

As I mentioned, you wouldn't want to do this at first. But for chronic problems, it may work well.

Christ was probably the first person to advocate changing people by going along with them. In His day, it was the custom for Roman soldiers and officials spontaneously to commandeer a Jew to carry the Roman's burden. This was an intolerable custom for the Jews, who already chafed under Roman rule. In the face of this resistance, Christ advocated a startling approach. "And whoever compels you to go one mile, go with him two" (Matt. 5:41). His other advice, to turn the other cheek or give your coat when a person asks for your cloak, were excellent illustrations of changing people by accommodating them (see Matt. 5:39–40). (It is good advice on how to change yourself, as well.)

One of the big advantages of the accommodation method is that it gets around the issue of self-acceptance. Anytime we try to change someone by opposing them, we are, in effect, saying that we don't accept them as they are. We are saying to the depressed person, "I won't fully accept you until you are cheerful again. I don't exactly like you the way you are now, and I want you to change."

Sometimes people oppose even needed changes because the very fact that we ask for them is hard on their self-esteem. In order to protect their self-esteem, they resist the change. They say to themselves, "This person doesn't like me the way I am, so he must not be my friend. He is hurting me so I'll withdraw from him and his suggestions and just protect myself."

By accommodating them, and even taking their weakness a step further, we avoid battles over self-esteem and yet, if we do it effectively, still get the message across that they need to change.

The third way that people change is through a *crisis*. Oftentimes a crisis is a "make or break" motivator. Most people do not enjoy going through a crisis. But unfortunately some changes are brought about only through crisis. Many people aren't motivated to change unless they have to; and crisis typically creates a strong need for change in order to resolve the conflict and tension.

Recently I counseled Brad, a man who had always had a tense relationship with his father. Brad grew up fearing his dad, a physically powerful and emotionally dominating man. Even after he reached adulthood, Brad walked on eggshells around his dad, dreading a confrontation with someone he viewed as so overwhelming. But when Brad was twenty-six he met and fell in love with a woman who was divorced and had a small child. Brad's father, whose religion strongly opposed divorce, threatened to disinherit Brad if he married this woman. He tried every psychological technique to bully Brad into abandoning this relationship. But Brad loved this woman so much that he set aside his fear of his father and stood right up to him. "I love Nancy, and I'm going to marry her, no matter what you say about it," he told his dad. Brad did marry Nancy, but his relationship with his dad did not disintegrate as he had anticipated. Brad had a new sense of confidence and independence, partly because of his marriage, but also because he found great satisfaction in conquering his fear of his dad. And his dad gained new respect for Brad and gradually developed a more relaxed and open relationship with him.

Psychologists have studied the role of conflict (a way crisis is created) in a variety of settings, such as industry, government, and families. Generally we think of conflict as a bad thing, but research indicates that it often plays a role in change and development, that the ability to experience conflict is an important component in the healthy organization or individual. Without conflict there is often no growth.

Among psychosomatic families, for example, conflict between husband and wife is avoided at all cost. The underlying tension and hostility may be so thick you could cut them with a knife, but husband and wife choose to act as if everything is fine, hoping that the bad feelings will miraculously disappear. Psychosomatic families are so named because they have at least one child with a psychosomatic disorder (a physical illness, such as recurrent diabetic acidosis, severe asthma, or anorexia nervosa, that was either caused or worsened by problems within the child's family).

One of the main features that psychologists have discovered in the psychosomatic family is a strong resistance to any type of conflict between husband and wife. Researchers who have watched psychosomatic families and normal families interact have found that husbands and wives in normal families engage in conflict much more often than husbands and wives in psychosomatic families. Spouses in the psychosomatic families don't disagree directly with each other. Instead, they communicate with each other through the child. This places the child under severe emotional stress—either creating or exacerbating an illness.

But because the husbands and wives in normal families have conflict doesn't mean they get overly emotional, throw things, or lose their tempers. They are willing to disagree with each other and express their disagreement. But they also listen to and acknowledge the other person's side. In other words, they are willing to have conflict, but they also have the maturity and techniques with which to *resolve* that conflict.

One reason why some people don't benefit more from conflict or crisis is because they have been raised to believe that all conflict is bad and that if you have a good relationship with a person you will always agree and get along with that person. "He must not love me anymore," a new bride will say to herself after a disagreement, "or we wouldn't have had that argument."

I have a friend, Bonnie, whose parents never had a disagreement in her presence. Her mom, a very accommodating woman, generally overlooked the flaws in her husband and accepted his criticism of her shortcomings without comment. So when Bonnie married, she expected her marriage to go much the same way. Bonnie had a problem, though—she was not easygoing like her mom. In fact, she was very sensitive to rejection and criticism. Bonnie's honeymoon was glorious; she and Chuck spent a week in the mountains, hiking, canoeing, and listening to the waterfalls. But the week they came home and moved into their new apartment, Bonnie and Chuck had their first real quarrel.

Bonnie had written a check without recording it in the checkbook, a pet peeve of Chuck's. To make matters worse, even though she knew to whom she had made out the check, Bonnie couldn't remember the exact amount. Chuck, who came from a family that dealt with problems very directly, told Bonnie exactly how he felt about the mistake. Bonnie was crushed and burst into tears. After Chuck finished telling her about his anger and frustration, she quietly went into the bedroom and started packing her suitcase. When Chuck came in to check on her, she was almost finished. "What in the world are you doing?" he asked in disbelief. "Well, since our marriage is over and you don't love me anymore," she replied, "I figured I'd better leave." She honestly believed that Chuck wanted to divorce her since he had been so direct in his criticism of her. She couldn't understand that he was merely venting his emotions and that he still loved her deeply. She had never experienced the closeness that the resolution of conflict can bring.

Often conflicts and crises are the very building blocks to growth. In fact, it seems to me that couples who live their lives together without ever growing or changing are many times those who either can't tolerate or don't know how to resolve crisis and conflict. Sometimes women endure their men's ego problems for years because they (the women) can't deal with conflict. (Often it's the husband who can't cope with conflict—change then involves an accommodation procedure.)

These three general approaches to change may be applied to several specific male ego problems that women most often said troubled them.

Criticism

One of the ego problems women mentioned most often was criticism. "My husband puts down everything I do. If he's not criticizing my cooking, then he's down on me about my looks. He says I talk too much and that I'm disorganized. There are so many things that I do wrong, I don't know which one to work on first. But the strange thing is, I can't say one negative thing about him or he gets his feelings hurt and won't speak to me for days."

It seems that some men have poor ego strength and that they criticize their wives in order to build themselves up. They feel dissatisfied with themselves and their own performance, but rather than face the issue squarely and try to bring about change in their own lives, they make themselves feel better momentarily by pointing out their wives' shortcomings. At the same time, they feel very vulnerable and hurt when their wives turn the tables on them and point out their weaknesses. Their already low self-esteem sinks even further.

Of course, some criticism is helpful, especially if given in a constructive manner; if you have an area that needs improvement, a person can do you a real service by pointing out your weakness and offering suggestions for change. In this case, the mature person listens with an open mind to the criticism, tries to understand and accept it, and, it is hoped, works to strengthen the weakness.

But what I am talking about here is not an isolated incident of criticism, but rather a person with a critical, faultfinding spirit. This is the husband who has a hard day at the office and automatically comes home and unloads on his wife, night after night. This is the father who thinks his children do nothing right, who shows them nothing but disdain and disapproval. This is the man who is impossible to please, no matter how hard you try. When a woman faces a situation like this, she usually requires some kind of coping strategy to help her maintain her own self-esteem. Without some technique to deal with constant criticism, she may develop her own problems with low self-esteem and eventually became a critical person herself.

This happened to Charlene, a woman who had been married to a critical man for almost twenty years. During their early married life, when Charlene's husband would berate her, she would beg his forgiveness and promise to do better. But he was displeased with so many things that eventually she realized that she could never suit him completely. So she started fighting fire with fire. If he criticized her cooking, she criticized his yard work. If he disliked her new hairdo, she would make derogatory remarks about his choice of clothing.

This drove such a wedge between them that eventually Charlene abandoned this practice, too. She felt completely helpless against his onslaught of faultfinding now, so she just gave up. She began to believe that her husband's criticism was justified, that she deserved it, and she finally saw herself through her husband's eyes—as a failure. Whereas before marriage she had been a cheerful, optimistic person who could conquer the world, now she felt so lacking in confidence that she couldn't do the simplest tasks. And in order to enhance the small amount of self-esteem she had left, Charlene started looking at the faults of others. "I'm not as sloppy as Jane or as disorganized as Peggy," she'd reason. She started criticizing other drivers on the street, entertainers on TV, the Post Office, the Red Cross, the Europeans, the Asians, the Africans. . . .

Charlene, like all other women who have to deal with excessively critical men, needed to learn an effective coping strategy. She needed to discover techniques she could utilize that would take the sting out of her husband's critical spirit without destroying her own self-esteem in the process.

Here are some techniques she might have tried:

1. *Write a letter.* Many people find it hard to have a direct confrontation with another person. Discussing an area of contention or hurt can be an uncomfortable task for all parties involved. A lot of people choose to put their feelings on paper in the form of a letter. You can

write to the person who is hurting you and tell him exactly how you feel. If Charlene had tried this approach, her letter might have gone something like this:

Dear Bud,

I am writing this letter because I love you dearly and because I feel that something is harming our relationship together. It makes me feel very bad when you criticize me. Because you are so important to me, I want to please you in every possible way. I understand that there are lots of ways I can improve as a wife and a mother, and I do want to be the best person I can be.

But I get discouraged when you put down so many things I do. When you criticize my cooking *and* my housekeeping *and* my appearance *and* my social skills, I don't know where to begin working. There are so many problem areas that I can't get the motivation to work on any of them.

Could you please give me encouragement instead of criticism? Instead of telling me, "These beans taste lousy," please say, "Why don't you try cooking the beans a little longer (or maybe try a little less salt)." It would make a world of difference to me, and I feel that our marriage would be a lot happier. And Bud, could you just mention one thing at a time? That would help a lot, too.

Your loving wife,

Charlene

Notice that Charlene's letter contains a lot of "I" messages: "I want to please you," "I get discouraged," "I feel hurt," "I can't get the motivation." You describe your reactions to the situation and avoid as much as possible pointing the finger at the other person's faults. This sort of letter can be a consciousness-raising experience for the other person, hopefully allowing him to see the situation from your point of view. You will seldom get a direct reply to your letter—the recipient might not ever mention it—but it should produce some positive results.

2. *Verbal confrontation.* For two people with secure egos and a good knowledge of "productive fighting," nothing beats a face-to-face verbal confrontation. Both parties get a chance to state their cases; both people have an opportunity to learn the other side of an issue. And ideally, before the confrontation is over, the conflict is resolved and feelings of harmony return.

Speaking to another person about very deep feelings—both positive and negative—comes more easily for some people than for others. If you grew up in a family where everything was out in the open, where issues were discussed and resolved, where feelings were accepted, then you have a real advantage over another person whose family kept all resentments, joys, and frustrations under the surface. So it's important to realize that verbal confrontation, while being an excellent technique, just won't work for everybody. A wife may feel compelled to clear the air and tell her husband exactly how she feels about some problem; but if her husband feels threatened by her words, then she does more harm than good for forcing the issue. So if you try verbal confrontation and meet a lot of resistance from the other person, it might be wise to try another strategy.

I have counseled with numerous husbands and wives who longed to talk to their spouses about problem areas in the family, only to have their mates throw up a stone wall of silent defensiveness when they tried. One couple I know almost wrecked their marriage over this issue. The husband was a very direct man; he said what he thought when he thought it. His wife, on the other hand, was a sensitive woman who, because of her family background, had never shared her inner feelings with anyone. If she felt angry, she tried to suppress her indignation. If she felt hurt, she kept it to herself. They had a stormy courtship but eventually got married.

The first six months of their marriage was a nightmare. If the husband would make a suggestion or discuss a problem, she considered it strong criticism because she'd never lived with anyone direct before. She would be crushed, lapsing into hours or days of silent hurt. When he tried to get her to talk about the problem, she refused. He felt totally frustrated, and she felt completely misunderstood and unloved. Fortunately a crisis in his family caused their separation for several weeks, and both husband and wife realized how much they truly loved each other. Their time apart provided a chance for hurts to heal so they could begin afresh, motivated to improve their relationship and their skills at communicating.

For those who are comfortable with a direct discussion of a problem, many of the ground rules are the same as for the letter. Use a lot of "I" messages and avoid attacking the other person. Instead of answering defensively "Well, of course I'm slow; you would be, too, if you had as much on your mind as I do," listen carefully to what the other person is saying. Try to see if you can understand his point of view. "I see what you're saying. . . . It makes you irritable when you have to wait thirty minutes for me to do a ten-minute job." And above all, strive to let the *relationship* win, rather than one person or the other. In marriage, if just one person wins, you both lose.

3. *Go with the Flow.* Sometimes letters and direct confrontation just don't get the job done. They may help the situation a little, but there's still lots of room for improvement. Then it's time to try another technique I'll call "go with the flow."

Sandy's husband had always been critical, but lately the situation was becoming unbearable. He loved to eat home-cooked meals—hot biscuits, fresh vegetables, home-made apple pie—and Sandy had always tried her best to prepare good meals for him. But now she was working full-time, and she just couldn't do as much elaborate cooking as she'd done before. Of course, he should have understood her dilemma and been a little more flexible in his desires—but he wasn't. He complained at nearly every meal; suppertime became a torture for Sandy. He criticized other areas in her life, too—she wasn't keeping the house clean; her hair was too short; she was too lenient with the children. There seemed no end to his complaints.

Sandy tried writing him a letter asking him to be less critical. She left it on the seat of his car so he'd be sure and see it. But he never mentioned the letter or its contents to her. "Oh, he did improve some," she told me. "He started taking me out to eat more often, and he stopped criticizing my hairdo. But in general, he still expressed a lot of dissatisfaction with me. I could never feel at ease around him because I was always afraid of what he'd find fault with."

Next Sandy tried verbal confrontation. "I told him how bad his criticism made me feel, and I begged him to really open up and share whatever hurt or frustration was making him do this. But he refused to talk to me about it. He told me, 'I've never discussed my deepest feelings with anyone, and I don't intend to start now. So please just leave me alone!' Then he sulked around for two or three days, hardly speaking to me. Finally I asked him to go to a marriage counselor, but he refused."

Sandy was just about at the end of her rope when she stumbled upon a new strategy. One day her husband was criticizing her housekeeping (for the fifth time that week), and she said, almost in desperation, "I hate to admit it, but you're right. I'm a real slob. I've never been able to keep the house clean and I guess I never will." He stood there in silence for a second, with a stunned and puzzled look on his face, and then he quickly reassured her, "Oh, honey, I didn't say it was that bad. I just wish you wouldn't leave your needlework all over the sofa."

Sandy quickly realized that she was on to something. She decided to try taking her husband's criticism, accepting it, and even embellishing it, without bitterness or sarcasm. The next time he commented on her leniency with the kids, she said, "You know, you've pointed out a real problem area for me. I've read so many books about disciplining kids, but I can't seem to act upon what I read. I love the kids with all my heart, but I guess I'm a real failure as a mother." Again her husband reassured her, "You're not a failure. You're a good mother. The kids sure know that you love them."

After several days Sandy's husband stopped reassuring her. If she met his criticism with self-condemnation, he would just walk away in silence. But slowly Sandy began to notice a real change in him. He was criticizing her far less often; and when he did find fault with her, he did so with much less enthusiasm.

"Going with the flow," as Sandy discovered, involves taking what someone else has said and elaborating on it, extending it, emphasizing it. This technique accepts the criticism being offered and adds, "It's even worse than you think!" Of course, you must show no hint of sarcasm or your efforts will backfire. But, properly delivered, this strategy takes all the "fun" out of criticism. It's almost as if you're saying, "You're not telling me anything I don't already know. I discovered this fault a long time ago, and I'll be glad to tell you all about it. I won't even get offended if you mention it; in fact, I'd love to talk about it." It's like calling up your friend with a juicy bit of news only to have your friend say, "Oh, that. Everybody in town knew that last week."

Blaming

Closely related to the man who criticizes is one who habitually blames others for mix-ups, mistakes, accidents, and hurt feelings. This is the man who, when he finds that something has gone wrong, instantly goes down a mental checklist to discover who is at fault. (It's never him, by the way—but women married to blamers already know that.) This is the man who leaves all the trip preparations—reservations, packing, supplies—up to his wife and then hits the ceiling if she forgets to pack his favorite T-shirt. This is the boss who gives incomplete instructions to his secretary and then tells her how disappointed he is when she doesn't read his mind and do everything exactly as he wanted. This is the father who constantly berates his son and then doesn't understand why the boy isn't highly motivated to succeed, and who blames his wife, or the teacher, or the school system, for his son's poor school grades.

The blamer habitually is on the lookout for mistakes and faults in others and is quick to jump on any sign of error. But occasionally he'll even set up other people so that he can blame them. In *Games People Play,* Eric Berne describes a man who loved to vent his wrath on anyone he caught in error. So when he needed some extensive plumbing work done, he went into excruciating detail with the plumber, describing exactly what needed to be done and establishing how much it would cost, down to the penny. He made a verbal agreement with the plumber that under no circumstances would the job go over the cost estimate agreed upon by the two men. Unfortunately, two-thirds of the way through the job, the plumber had to install an extra valve, which cost about four dollars.

When the plumber submitted his bill, he charged the original figure plus four dollars for the unexpected valve. The man flew into a rage the minute he saw the bill. He accused the plumber of unethical behavior and dishonesty, insulted his business practices, and even criticized the plumber's lifestyle. After repeated phone calls and a letter, the plumber finally gave in and withdrew the four-dollar charge. But the man's main objective had already been accomplished; he had discharged pent-up fury on a victim who had made a trivial mistake.

You can handle the blamer in much the same way that you deal with the critical man. Writing a letter and direct confrontation may both help. But "going with the flow" could be one of your best strategies. This steals the blamer's thunder. He loves to point out how it's all your fault, especially if you defend yourself; then he has the opportunity to present his evidence all over again with renewed vigor. But if you agree that you're at fault, if you accept all the blame, then there's nothing left for him to say.

A friend of mine named Dick discovered this principle in an interaction with his blamer father. His father asked him if he had cleaned out the car, and Dick, who had been busy studying for a test, started to defend himself. "Well, no, Dad, I. . . ." Dick never finished his sentence because his father jumped in: "You said you'd have it done by now. What happened? You told me plainly you'd have the car clean by this afternoon!" Dick, who couldn't remember making any such promise, replied cooly, "Well, I lied." His father stood there in stunned silence and has never mentioned the incident again.

Since blamers are very difficult to change, it is often a good idea to develop a sense of humor in dealing with them. You'll never be arrested or imprisoned for being twenty minutes late or forgetful or messy, so why not accept the blame and heap even more of it on yourself? If your husband says, "You said you'd be here at 2:00 and you got here at 2:15," then why not retort somewhat cheerfully, "Well, I'm just incompetent. I guess I'll never be able to change my poor shoddy habits. And I never did learn to tell time well."

Another way to interject humor into an interaction with a blamer is to have him rate the degree of your guilt, "Boy, I didn't realize how bad it was. Maybe you ought to be more specific. How much of this was my fault—where do I rate on a scale of one to ten?" Of course, it helps if the blamer has a sense of humor, too!

The Man Who Can't Take Criticism

Frequently the man who makes a habit of criticizing or blaming is unable to take criticism himself. As I stated earlier, one reason he looks critically at others is to boost his sagging ego. The last thing he wants to hear is a disparaging remark about himself.

But sometimes it becomes necessary to tell him something negative, and it helps to know the most positive way to do so. It still won't be any fun for him to take the medicine, but at least the sugar-coating will make it go down more easily.

In general, the most effective way to deliver criticism to anyone is to give "I feel" messages instead of "you" messages. Rather than saying, "You hurt my feelings," say, "I was really hurt when you said. . . ." Concentrate on your feelings rather than the other person's actions: "I'm confused," "I'm angry," "I feel put down." People can't really argue with your feelings, because they are uniquely your own.

With the man who can't take criticism, perhaps the best strategy is to write a letter using the "I" messages. Here, too, you would want to make the letter as positive as possible. Instead of saying, "You did . . . ," write, "Would you mind trying . . . ?" In other words, don't condemn the action you don't like; rather, ask the person to do the opposite of that behavior.

A small boy came in for counseling because he habitually bit his own hand. The situation had become so bad that he'd had over twenty stitches to close the wounds he had made. The counselor had two choices: either he could use electrical shock to the boy's hand every time he put it near his mouth, or he could reward him for keeping his hand at his side, a behavior incompatible with the biting. The counselor chose the latter method, a much more positive strategy.

This may also be done with the person who can't take criticism. If a man is very negative, rather than tell him, "You're very negative," ask him to try being more positive. If he doesn't spend time with the children, explain your concerns about the children needing a male image ("You know, I'm afraid Jimmy is around women too much. He is always wanting to put on make-up and wear my high heels"), and then ask him if he could take some extra time with his son. ("I bet it would mean a lot to him to go someplace special with you. Could you possibly take him to the ice cream parlor for a few minutes tomorrow? I know he'd really enjoy that.")

Most behaviors are on a continuum with a negative and positive end. For example, "sloppy" is the negative opposite of "neat," "dishonest" is the negative opposite of "honest," "uninterested" is opposite to "involved," and so on. Thus, when you are confronted with a negative trait, try to suggest the positive rather than condemn the negative. If the person follows your suggestion, it will automatically eliminate the negative without the two of you having to go through the ego problems that often result from negativism and criticism.

Extreme Desire for Control

Another ego problem that women mentioned frequently was their men's overzealous quest for control. Some women must contend with men who need every aspect of their environment regulated down to the smallest detail. Their shoes must be lined up according to color; the kitchen must always be spotless; dinner must be served promptly at six o'clock; there must be no surprises.

I talked recently to an interior decorator who had worked for just such a man. He was single and buying his first house. She was very excited about working with him because he had virtually no furniture and was starting from scratch. She thought she could help him put together a really well-coordinated home. But it wasn't long before she realized that he was rejecting all her suggestions. He knew *exactly* what he wanted for every room in the house. He even vetoed her idea about hanging the wallpaper a certain way. He wanted total control over his environment, and all her efforts were fruitless.

Frequently these needs extend beyond the external environment of the home. Often a man's desire for control is expressed in his feelings about getting married, changing jobs, or having children. He approaches major life changes with great caution and care. He will not be pushed or hurried into anything so important. As a result many women express frustration over their men's reluctance to set a wedding date or to agree on having a child: "I want very much to have a baby, but my husband keeps putting me off. He is perfectly contented with our life together and can't understand my desire for a child. He says, 'Wait until I get a promotion,' or 'Maybe after we get the car paid off,' or 'Not until we've bought a house.' Why doesn't he want a family, too?"

Marriage, a new job, or a baby (especially the first) present real threats to the controlling man. He cannot be sure how these changes will affect his lifestyle. They represent a source of ambiguity and loss of control to him. So he avoids them, or at least approaches them with extreme caution. This is especially true in the case of firstborn males who contemplate having children. These men were usurped one time long ago by younger siblings, and they don't wish to repeat this unsettling experience.

Another area in which men display this need to control their lives is in their reluctance to seek help from other men. One wife told me, "My husband, my dad, and my father-in-law all refuse to ask for directions when they're lost. They would rather drive thirty miles out of the way than admit they need help." Judging from the interviews we did for this book, hers is a common complaint. Many men just don't like to turn over control of their lives to anyone, even in a trivial matter. It is very difficult for them to feel dependent on another person. This is also reflected in the fact that men go to physicians, psychotherapists, and marriage counselors much less often than do women. I have known several men personally who have died because they postponed going to the doctor until it was too late. And some men would rather face divorce than let a marriage counselor tell them what to do to make their marriage work.

There is a small bit of irony, though, in this tendency of men to cherish independence. Many men think nothing of turning over nearly all the errands in their personal lives to their wives or secretaries. A man who would never ask a friend for advice about a problem with his wife will tell his secretary, "Pick out a birthday present for my wife. I don't care what you get. You know more about what women like than I do. Would you have it wrapped and pick out a card, too?" Men, it seems, can tolerate dependence very well if they can call the shots, if they become dependent by choice rather than by necessity. It is when external control or direction is thrust upon them by circumstances that they rebel against it.

Women through the ages have discovered a subtle technique to make this irony in men work to their advantage. As one woman put it, "My mom taught me long ago that men find it hard to take suggestions from women. She told me that I should plant an idea in my husband's mind and then drop it. After a few days he usually adopts the idea as his own and follows through on it. This is definitely the best way to get a man to do what you suggest."

This woman and countless others have found that this technique works quite well as long as you make the suggestion once and then let the man take over. (I am assuming that the idea is one with which he can basically agree. If it's not, he will rightly see your use of this technique as an attempt to manipulate him.) This gives him the feeling of being in control of the situation while you still have the satisfaction of having your idea acted upon. But if you start thinking, "Maybe he didn't hear me," or "Maybe he misunderstood," and bring it up again, he'll see this as nagging or an intrusion into his territory. It will end up like my daughter's science project.

Since Jessica's class was studying plants, her teacher brought a package of lima bean seeds to school one day, along with a bag of potting soil and some plastic cups. The children each planted four seeds, watered them, and set them in the window to grow. Several of the children's seeds sprouted right away and grew plants over two inches tall by the time of the science fair. But most of the seeds were a little slower, not even cracking the surface of the dirt on the appointed date. Jessica and her friends with the tardy seeds chose to take action; they decided to help their seeds along by digging them up and replanting them. But in the process, they killed the fragile new plant life under the soil. I hope the analogy is clear: if you plant your idea in your husband's mind, don't keep "digging it up" to see how it's progressing. Leave it alone so it will have time to grow and flourish.

Of course, the need for control varies from man to man. Some are like Max, who has an obsessive desire to oversee everything remotely connected to him just for sheer love of control. He plans the menus for his wife, inspects the kitchen after the dishes are washed, stands beside his children while they do their homework, and writes out a list of instructions for the feeding and confinement of the dog. If anything in his environment goes wrong—if the dog chews up a pillow or his child brings home lower grades than usual—he takes drastic action.

Other men prefer to keep a looser hold on things. Frequently they like to have their home lives well-ordered and running smoothly, so that home can be a refuge from the stress of the working world; but they leave the details up to their wives. These men are generally very job-oriented. Their egos are dependent on work; and they need their wives to manage the home environment so that it can serve as a place, not to drain their energies, but to recharge their batteries, so to speak.

There are still other men who exercise a different form of control. These men have a lot of ego invested in their image, in the way the world views them. They expend much energy in the quest for the best-decorated home, the most immaculate lawn, the most expensive clothing, and the most status-enhancing wife. These men will exert a very strong influence on their women, urging them to attain a high education, a more stylish appearance, or a more prestigious job—depending, of course, on what the man himself values and the image he seeks to project. An acquaintance of mine told his wife several months before their marriage, "I expect you to continue working until you reach retirement age so that we can maintain the lifestyle I want." He overruled her desire for children so that she could get advanced degrees and a more prestigious job.

So the desire for control seems to be found frequently and among many types of men. If it is carried to an extreme, the best strategy is to sit down and talk about it, calmly and rationally. Although I seriously doubt that many men will ever give up this need for control altogether, they can frequently alter their behavior after a reasonable discussion about it. Sometimes you find that even when discussions don't bring about an immediate result, a seed will be planted and, if allowed to grow undisturbed, will result in improved behavior. Unfortunately, people often tend to get discouraged when there are no sudden changes; they start to complain or nag, and the man resists their efforts. But once a man gets over the pain of receiving a suggestion or criticism, if not nagged about it, he'll forget the source of it, take it as his own, see the fairness of it, and subsequently change his behavior.

Jealousy

A third male ego problem that women often mentioned was jealousy. Many men, it seems, want their wives' or girlfriends' undivided attention and adoration; they resent having to share their women with anyone or anything.

One woman, Maxine, told me about her husband, Joe's, possessiveness and jealousy when they were first wed. Joe was drafted into the army only six months after they married. He was sent halfway across the country for basic training and was not even allowed off the base for the first few months. Maxine stayed home to work as a receptionist until she could join Joe at a permanent assignment. Joe called home every night and talked to Maxine anywhere from thirty minutes to two hours each time. Whenever she mentioned that a girlfriend had invited her out to eat supper or that a family asked if she could accompany them to a baseball game, Joe would tell her not to go. He wanted her right by the phone when he called.

Male jealousy comes in two basic forms—general jealousy and sexual jealousy. General jealousy is the resentment that men experience over anything that takes their women's attention away from them. This is the kind of jealousy that Joe displayed toward Maxine.

Judging from the interviews done for this book, many men have these feelings. Over and over again, women would tell us, "My husband never acts worse than when we have company. My usually thoughtful and considerate man becomes sullen and withdrawn whenever people visit for a day or two. It's like he's punishing me for not giving him enough attention."

Several women also noticed that their men got more demanding: "Lester knows that I'm in the kitchen, working as hard as I can to get supper ready; but he'll call me into the living room to ask me a question, to show me a funny scene on TV, or just to ask for a drink of water. Of course, the most embarrassing situation arises when he wants me to drop everything and make love in the middle of the day. I have to explain to my guests why they won't be seeing either of us for a while, without turning several shades of red."

Male jealousy shows itself on many occasions other than in the presence of house guests. Some men show resentment not only of other people, but also of activities. One woman commented, "My husband wants my undivided attention while I am talking to him. I must look right at him, too. This means no needlework or crafts, no washing dishes, etc. I have a great time with my girlfriends as we work together and talk at the same time. The kids bounce in and out, and we still chat away. Why does it have to be so different with my husband?"

Men like to be first in the lives of their women. They don't want anything to dethrone them from that position of primary importance. Never is this more apparent than in the reaction men have to the birth of their first child. With the birth of his first child, every man comes to realize that never again will he be the most important person in another individual's eyes; he feels a loss and a frustration at having to share what was formerly his alone. Men react to these feelings in various ways: some begin drinking heavily and stay away from home for long periods of time; some of them get surly and begin to resent their own children; some withdraw emotionally from the marital relationship; some throw themselves into their work with renewed vigor.

Jack's daughter was born after he and Nancy had been married for seven years. He went with Nancy into the delivery room and held his little girl even before his wife did. He felt so much pride, joy, and awe as he held that perfect little baby in his arms that he couldn't imagine ever having a negative thought about her. But by the time she was six weeks old, Jack was having second thoughts. "I love her as much as is humanly possible," he'd tell himself, "but she has really put a cramp in our marital lifestyle. Nancy doesn't have time to have deep conversations with me anymore; she doesn't even cook breakfast for me in the morning!"

Jack became increasingly frustrated, especially as he realized that his little "bundle of joy" was going to require Nancy's full attention for quite some time. But fortunately he decided to make the best of the situation and use all this extra time he suddenly had on his hands—time he used to spend with Nancy—to pursue a long-held goal.

Ever since Jack had taken art in college, he had wanted to paint. So he went out and bought an easel, some paints, and a canvas and set to work. Before long his paintings improved so much that he decided to take them to neighborhood art shows. He met with surprising success here, too, and soon the money from his art work was providing a good supplement to his regular income as well as giving him additional prestige at his job.

Jack was fortunate to cope with his jealousy in a constructive way. But what if your husband shows no such good judgment? What if he comes home late four or five nights a week? What if he acts resentful toward you and the new baby, too? What if he becomes sullen and withdrawn and won't discuss his feelings with you?

Here are several ideas women often find helpful when dealing with men who display jealousy.

1. Look at the jealousy from a positive point of view.

Don't feel threatened by it. In essence, by showing jealousy your man is saying, "You are important to me, and I need you. I resent anything that might possibly endanger the relationship we now have. I value your companionship and the attention you give me."

I talked with one woman whose husband showed a great deal of possessiveness toward her and her time. He didn't want her to wash dishes after supper; rather he asked her to come and sit with him so they could watch the news together. He often interrupted her other housework because he wanted to talk. And he even called her at work at least once a week to see if she could have lunch with him. Since she was a task-oriented person, these frequent interruptions really got on her nerves. She'd hear women complain about how their husbands never talked with them, and she'd say to herself, "They should be counting their blessings. At least they can get something done." But eventually her husband got so involved with his career that he had less and less time to spend with her. She had plenty of opportunity to get her work done, but she felt strangely dissatisfied. Finally it occurred to her that she actually missed all the interaction with her husband. It had become an important part of her life, and she felt a little empty without it.

2. If your man's display of jealousy revolves around his desire for your attention, then one of your best strategies would be to give him the undivided attention he values so much. Set aside time to sit down and talk with him—no TV, no needlework, no newspapers—just one-to-one interaction. If you have small children, take them to a babysitter or friend's house and go out together, just the two of you. If you are like many women I've talked

to, you will gradually learn to appreciate the intimacy that these conversations bring as much as your man does.

But what if your man doesn't like to talk; what if he just wants you nearby while he's working on the car or watching the ballgame? You can probably learn to enjoy interacting with him in this way, too, especially when you realize how much these self-sacrificing actions mean for your relationship together.

Some men, besides showing a general jealousy of their women's activities, become very sensitive to the way their wives or girlfriends relate to other men. Such a man gets enraged if it appears his wife is flirting with another man, or even if she seems too interested in talking to him. He suspects that every man his wife mentions might be a potential threat to their marriage. He is on the lookout for any signs of disloyalty or unfaithfulness in his wife.

Generally the man who has this sort of extreme distrust of his woman fits into one of two categories. Either his woman is giving him some reason to suspect her ("She says she just doesn't love me anymore. She refuses to have sexual relations with me, and yet she takes birth control pills every day") or the man has a troubled background, which would lead him to distrust women.

Brett fit into the second category. He and his wife Sue came to my office because of marital problems. Sue felt bored and isolated at home and wanted to work; but every time she'd get a job that she really liked, Brett would fume and fuss and pick at her until she quit. And his complaints were nearly always about the men she worked with. "I've seen the way you and Bill look at

[157]

each other when you think I'm not watching. You've got something going with him, don't you?" No matter how much Sue denied his accusations, she could not convince him of her love and loyalty. So eventually she would resign and get another job. By the time they came to my office, Sue was on her fourth job, and Brett's jealousy had gotten so bad that he even suspected Sue's doctor, her dentist, and the vet.

It didn't take long to uncover the source of Brett's mistrust. He told me that his earliest memories of his mother were of her short-lived liaisons with a string of boyfriends, none of whom stayed around for more than a few months at a time. Brett had no permanent father figure, and his primary relationship with a woman—his mother—was marred by her promiscuity and instability. To make matters worse, Brett's sister became a prostitute while still a teen-ager and made no effort to hide her activities from him. So Brett grew up with a deep-seated insecurity about women, especially about their ability to remain loyal to one man.

Situations like Brett's require help far beyond the scope of this kind of book. If your man shows extreme jealousy without cause, or shows jealousy toward nearly every man in your life, he might need professional counseling by a qualified therapist.

The Nonexpressive Male

Here we have one of the most common ego problems women must endure in their men: lack of communication. It comes in several forms—no display of interest ("My husband walks out of the room while I'm talking to him"); refusing to talk ("There's a lot of tension in our marriage, but when I try to get my husband to discuss our problems, he gets angry and says it won't help a thing"); lack of intimacy ("We just don't have anything to talk about since the kids have left home. I try to carry on conversations with my husband, but it's just a monologue. He doesn't contribute a thing").

Most women love to communicate. They like nothing better than a deep conversation with a close friend. Nothing seems to satisfy their needs in quite the same way. So they are particularly troubled by men who see no value in sharing.

Pam and Bill, a couple I knew several years ago, were deeply committed to each other and to their two children. But Pam lived on the brink of emotional disaster because Bill was uncommunicative. Pam experienced life deeply; she regularly climbed the mountaintops of joy and descended into the valleys of despair. It was not at all unusual for her to start crying in the middle of a conversation. Bill, on the other hand, was extremely patient and easygoing. He would have been the perfect balance for Pam's emotionality except that he just wouldn't take the time to talk with her. He would come home from work each night and go directly to the bedroom to "unwind." He would eat supper in front of the TV and then read professional journals until bedtime. To have any kind of meaningful conversation at all, Pam had to make an appointment with Bill. "I need to talk to you about something," she'd say. "When can you sit down and discuss this?" She saved her "appointments" for very crucial conversations and let the rest of her sharing with Bill slide. But, still, she had to release her pent-up emotions regularly by crying, talking to a friend, or vigorous exercise.

Not all women react like Pam. Some become uncommunicative themselves as a form of self-defense against the hurt of a nonsharing man. This happened to Suzanne. She married Tony right after she graduated from high school. She came from a close-knit family who shared almost everything with each other; and this was the kind of relationship she expected with her new husband. Tony, however, showed no need for emotional intimacy. He was perfectly content to laugh and joke with her, to discuss the weather, or the neighbor's new dog; but he grew strangely aloof and distant if Suzanne tried to tell him about her feelings. So she started keeping her deepest thoughts and emotions to herself. She held them tight, almost using them as a shield against Tony's distant, superficial manner. Eventually she grew fairly comfortable living with Tony, not really knowing him; but their marriage suffered since little frustrations, hurts, and aggravations were never cleared up. Suzanne and Tony are still married today; but their marriage is, in many ways, a joyless one.

Clearly, lack of communication and the failure to express feelings can deeply wound a marriage. What causes this problem and what can be done about it? The usual explanation is that men are socialized to keep their feelings to themselves. Little boys are taught to be brave and not to cry; men are expected to be strong and steady as a rock. Undoubtedly early training and cultural expectations do play a role in the reluctance of men to express their emotions, but there are other factors at work, too. Most men strive for control in their environment. They find it very upsetting if they walk in the door after work only to see things out of control— the house a mess, no food prepared, and the wife and children gone. At work they feel more comfortable if they have their own secretary rather than having to take their chances in a secretarial pool where their typing might or might not get done on time. Being in control gives men a feeling of security and peace of mind, while loss of control can generate more negative emotions such as irritability and anxiety over their importance in the scheme of things.

So control plays an important role in the life of men. They have to bridle many of their sexual and aggressive urges, and they value a controlled environment. Control of emotions, then, especially the outward display of feelings, fits right in with a man's general outlook on life.

Sometimes men are so convinced of the benefits of self-control that they fail to see the value of open expression even if it leaps out at them. Chris was having some problems at work. His boss had become increasingly critical of his management techniques, and rumors had spread over the office that a big organizational shake-up was at hand. Chris feared for his job; he couldn't even enjoy going home at night because he was reminded of all he might lose along with his job—his house, his boat, his new car.

Chris's wife, Janet, noticed right away that he felt deeply troubled about something; but when she asked him about it, he just told her, "There's nothing wrong. It's all your imagination." Janet began dreaming up all kinds of reasons why Chris was acting so strangely. *Maybe he's upset because I've been spending too much money lately. No, that's not it. Maybe I hurt him unintentionally at the beach last weekend. What could I have said?* Finally she couldn't stand the tension any longer so she asked again, "Chris, what is bothering you? Won't you please talk about it?"

Chris's emotions had about reached a breaking point so he delivered a tirade to Janet, telling her how useless talking would be. He accused her of harassing him and nagging him to talk when all he wanted was to be left alone. He spewed out all his negative reactions for fifteen minutes and then strolled out of the house, feeling much better. The very act of venting his frustration, wrath, and anxiety—even if he did it by telling Janet how useless such behavior was—helped Chris to cope with his problems at work.

Janet had inadvertently discovered one way of dealing with a nonexpressive male—create a crisis. Sometimes women have to force an issue out into the open and then endure a few minutes of unpleasantness in order to improve a situation. And if your man just doesn't know how, or won't communicate, you might really have to let your feelings out—even yell a little to show him how frustrated you are—in order to motivate him.

You might also want to try the "educational" approach. Be on the lookout for articles, books, and letters to Ann Landers describing the importance of communication. Then leave these materials lying around the house in strategic locations, never mentioning them otherwise, of course. Eventually your man may get the idea.

This system worked beautifully for a friend of our family named Jodie. She is a vivacious, joy-filled lady who practically explodes with energy and enthusiasm. She dearly loves her husband, but for many years she had to struggle with his lack of expression. When he would come home from work, she'd dash out to meet him, throw her arms around him, and give him an enthusiastic greeting. But he could barely manage, "Hi, honey."

One day Jodie's ebullience got the best of her, and she went into his bathroom while her husband was at work and wrote I LOVE YOU across the mirror in bright red lipstick. That evening he came home, his usual quiet self, and went to the bathroom to change clothes. He came out a second later with a big smile on his face and told Jodie, "I got your message." She was so encouraged by his reaction that she started leaving notes on his bathroom mirror every day. (She put them on notecards after the initial message—it took her two hours to get the lipstick off.) She noticed right away that her husband developed a habit of going to the bathroom as soon as he came home from work just to read the messages. And gradually he started showing Jodie love in new and wonderful ways. He began sending her cards once or twice a week; he brought her candy and flowers. He just looked for ways to express his love for her.

It would be wonderful if all men responded like Jodie's husband did; but some won't, so another strategy might be in order. Some men become so accustomed to their wives' warmth and expressiveness (and their own lack of the same) that they take the situation for granted. They just expect their women to respond positively to them, and it never crosses their minds that things might go differently. In situations like this, a woman might have to temporarily pull back emotionally to motivate her husband to express himself.

I counseled a wife and mother named Beth who exuded warmth and acceptance. Like Jodie, she always had a good word and plenty of affection for her husband. But her husband, Randy, wanted more distance than she did. He felt more comfortable with less intimacy, less sharing of feelings. So Beth decided to try an experiment: for one week she tried pulling back emotionally from him. She acted happy and content with herself, but was cheerfully distant. After the week was over, she came to my office and told me that he was really noticing the change in her and becoming a little insecure about it. In fact, this insecurity was motivating him to become more expressive himself as he tried to get her to return to her former warmth.

If all these techniques fail to help a man open up, a woman still has one option open to her. She can turn to her friends. Sometimes a woman just can't get the type of communication she wants in marriage, but generally she can find at least one female friend who will be glad to establish a close, sharing relationship with her. No man can empathize with postpartum depression (the "after-birth blues"). Few men can relate to the frustration of dealing with a negative child fourteen hours a day, seven days a week. And men rarely like to shop, decorate a house, or take aerobic dancing. But women can share all these experiences and more, while at the same time building a strong emotional bond that will ease the void left by a nonexpressive male.

The Depressed Male

Evelyn attended a women's Bible class the other day, and the subject of male depression came up. One woman's husband was despondent and discouraged, and she just didn't know how to cope with it. Surprisingly, each woman there could offer sympathy and encouragement, because each of them had witnessed their own husbands battle depression some time in the past. Each woman knew how helpless and frustrated she felt when all her efforts to help her husband proved fruitless.

Depression is a widespread problem today, among both men and women. Some men suffer depression because of an obvious event, such as the loss of a job. Other men seem naturally moody and prone to periodic low spells, with some lows lasting only a few hours and others lasting for months.

But whatever the source of your man's depression, the first thing to do for him is to encourage him and try to cheer him up. Point out to him the positive things in his life—his health, his creativity, his resourcefulness, his character, for example. Tell him that you are behind him and that you believe in him; give him emotional support in every way possible. And by all means let him talk if he will. Voicing the pain, anger, or hopelessness he feels may help these emotions ease up, at least temporarily.

Sometimes a man can recover from depression solely through the efforts of his loved ones. I read recently about a man who received a demotion and cut in pay at work, an event that would cause hurt and humiliation for any man. He subsequently developed a deep depression, in part as a natural result of his feelings of loss, but also as an attempt to test his family's love and loyalty to him. He felt less than worthwhile because of his demotion at work, and unconsciously he wanted to see if his family still valued him.

Fortunately this man's wife and children rallied around him, trying their best to please him and cheer him up. His wife cooked his favorite meals and spent a lot of time rubbing his back or watching TV with him. The children made a special effort to tell him about their experiences at school each day; and the family as a whole purposefully continued certain rituals which were carried over from happier times: his daughter brought him the paper every evening; his wife made him pizza every Saturday; and the whole family ate a leisurely pancake supper together each Sunday night. The man felt very reassured and confident about his importance in the family and gradually overcame his depression.

But sometimes, when the depression continues for months despite your persistent effort at support and encouragement, you may actually be affirming your man in his problems. In other words, he may have settled into a rut of depression, and you are unknowingly helping him stay there. Perhaps your best clue that this is happening may be when you regularly feel helpless and frustrated yourself. When *you* start to feel consistently defeated, then you can try a new strategy. Allow yourself to express your own sadness and pessimism.

Most families operate in a state of complementary balance. If one partner acts especially helpless, the other will become more competent to compensate for his mate. If one partner acts depressed, the other will become more cheerful. So a wife's persistent good spirits may allow the husband to continue his low mood, because that way the family stays in balance. If, on the other hand, the wife who feels genuinely depressed herself because of her husband's prolonged low period, expresses her feelings rather than covering them up, then the husband may be forced to cheer up so that he can help his wife. If he remains depressed while his wife also feels low, then the family will be out of balance; it will not feel psychologically "right."

So the very act of trying to cheer up a dispirited wife might bring a man out of his depression. Not only would he start behaving in a way not compatible with depression (cheerfully), but he would also be showing his own competence to handle an emotional problem. Often the feeling of incompetence is a big part of male depression, so getting him to behave competently might turn his mood around.

A woman, then, might want to express her own low emotions and her feelings of helplessness, too, especially if she has become supercompetent during her man's depression. She could ask him to help her in little ways: "I just can't figure out what's wrong with the car. I feel so frustrated! Could you check it out for me?"

This happened spontaneously with a couple I am counseling. He had been a successful business executive, but retired to take a part-time job. Unfortunately his job didn't work out so he began to look for other part-time employment. He finally found a position as a shoe salesman. His wife thought he'd be very happy to have a job, but instead he developed a depression. The job selling shoes was such a step down in status from his other work that he felt a profound loss. His wife just couldn't handle his depression. She felt totally helpless to cope with all the extra demands his low spirits and lack of motivation placed on her. She felt especially frustrated about the family finances. Finally she told him, "I don't want to pay the bills anymore. I can't seem to remember to pay them on time; and if I do, I end up paying some of them twice. It's just too confusing when companies send us an invoice and then a separate bill. Can't you take over this responsibility again, because it's killing me!" Her husband did resume paying the bills and began coming out of his depression, too, as he demonstrated his competence.

Part II

FOR MEN WHO WANT
MORE SECURE EGOS

NINE

Self-worth and the
Meaning of Masculinity

The goal of this part of the book is to encourage men to develop a stronger, more secure ego. This seems to be what women want for their men (perhaps so that they, the women, can be relieved of some of the responsibility for the male ego) and what men want for themselves.

I feel compelled to acknowledge, however, that for most men a certain amount of ego insecurity will always prevail. This is inherent in man's nature and in his relationship with women.

Self-worth and Self-esteem

Although men in all cultures share quite a few ego experiences, some important differences exist in the way men define and evaluate their own masculinity. Those definitions of masculinity have an impact on a man's level of self-esteem. If a man lived in a culture where his primary role consisted of constructing and playing song flutes, then he might have a very high level of self-esteem as he sat under the trees every day with his friends whittling on wood, fashioning and perfecting his flutes. In our culture, however, many men would experience ego-deflation if this were their most meaningful activity in life. Different cultures set up various roles for men, and a man's ego strength and self-esteem depend on how well he fills that role.

Self-esteem is a complex experience. It has been defined in a variety of ways and measured by a variety of tests. Probably the simplest and most straightforward definition of self-esteem is the following: self-esteem is an emotional attitude that you have about your own self. The fact that it is an attitude indicates that self-esteem depends in part on what you *think* about yourself. ("I *think* I am fairly successful at my job. I have received regular promotions, and my boss says he is pleased with my work.") But I am emphasizing an *emotional* experience when I talk about self-esteem—the positive, negative, or ambivalent feelings that you have toward yourself. ("Even though I am doing well at work, I *feel* as though I should do better. My dad had achieved financial independence at my age. Somehow I'm not quite satisfied with my progress.")

How much, then, does your thinking have to do with your self-esteem? The answer is, a lot. The way you think about yourself strongly influences the way you feel about yourself. But the thinking part has more to do with what I call self-worth than with self-esteem. If self-esteem is more of an emotional attitude about yourself, then self-worth is the intellectual part of your ego. Now for most people, this distinction between self-esteem and self-worth may seem irrelevant. And I must admit that when I'm counseling I tend to use the two terms interchangeably. But there is a fine distinction between the two.

In general I've found that six factors influence high self-esteem:

1. *Love and acceptance by parents.* If a man's parents

showed him genuine love and acceptance during his childhood, then he generally will feel good about himself. On the other hand, if his parents couldn't accept him as he was, or withheld love as a form of punishment, he may develop problems with insecurity and have to look for love and approval from others as a means of establishing healthy self-esteem.

2. *Personal resources.* High self-esteem is enhanced if a person possesses talents, skills, abilities, and attributes that society values. A handsome young football star who makes straight A's will generally have higher self-esteem than an acne-plagued, uncoordinated fellow who can barely pass remedial reading.

3. *Temperament.* Introverts (especially those with the "sensitive" personality style) generally have lower self-esteem than extroverts.

4. *Sense of self-worth.* The value or importance you place on yourself depends on what you value in others or what you consider makes a person worthwhile in general. I'll cover five different definitions of masculine self-worth in this chapter.

5. *Sense of self-respect.* Self-respect is probably best defined as the extent to which you are living up to your own standards and values. For example, if you are walking along a city street and see a woman being attacked and screaming for help and you respond by simply walking on and doing nothing, your self-respect will probably plummet.

6. *Beliefs and interpretations of events.* Your beliefs and assumptions about other people and about yourself mold the way you interpret your experiences. Those interpretations in turn help determine your level of self-esteem.

All of these six factors contribute to self-esteem. But

you only have control over the last three, especially self-worth.

Self-worth is too complex an issue to discuss in full here. But I do want to make an important point about self-esteem and self-worth: *I believe that we have more potential to change our level of self-esteem, and hence to develop a more secure ego, by changing our self-worth than by trying to change our self-esteem directly.* In other words, self-worth is easier to improve than self-esteem. And of the two, *self-worth is the more important ego component.*

One of the reasons why self-worth is so important is that it's a product, in part, of how you define human beings in general; in other words, it's a product of your philosophy of the meaning and importance of life.

Time after time in counseling I see people who have a poor feeling of self-worth, not because they don't have a lot going for them, but rather for the simple reason that they have a faulty definition or philosophy of self-worth. Since definitions and philosophies are much easier to change than emotional experiences, I've had better success in changing my clients' self-worth first than in trying to deal initially with their self-esteem. Of course, as the sense of self-worth improves, self-esteem automatically increases.

Robert Porter came to see me because he was having problems at work. He was unable to concentrate on the job at hand, and the harder he tried to do well, the more anxious and inefficient he became. As we discussed Robert's life situation, I discovered that he had a very aggressive, critical, and domineering father who had expected him to be an aggressive person from adolescence onward. When Robert did not display the kind of dynamic personality he hoped for, his father would belittle and ridicule him, trying to force Robert to show some of the aggression he longed to see. Robert, a sensitive and creative man, responded by becoming more withdrawn and silently hostile. His self-esteem plummeted because he could not live up to his father's expectations.

When I asked Robert how he pictured the ideal man, he drew a complete blank. The only man to whom he had been close was his father, and he certainly didn't consider his behavior ideal. Nevertheless, Robert had always compared his behavior to that of his father, had always tried to be like him, and had always come up short. When I went over the many strengths of the sensitive man with Robert, he saw for the first time that he was a unique individual, entirely different from his father, with completely different strengths and weaknesses, but with great potential for growth and productivity.

Once I convinced Robert's *mind* that he could make as great a contribution to society in his own way as had his father, then his *feelings* about himself began to change. He cared less and less about adopting his father's traits and began to appreciate his own attributes. He began to feel good about who he was and what he could do for the world, without degrading himself because he'd never be like his dad.

Self-worth and Masculinity

How do you measure self-worth? That's a difficult question to answer. We can measure specific traits like intelligence, height, and self-esteem; but we can't really measure self-worth as a separate entity.

How do you assess how much a human being is worth? Here again we have no strong guidelines on which everyone can agree. To a large extent, people have to choose their own criteria of self-worth. What are your standards for evaluating human beings? Some people look for strong character; others value a likable personality. Some may look at achievements; others at relationships, religious commitment, or education.

Whatever criteria you employ to evaluate human worth, those are the criteria you will use to assess your own self-worth. If you think that people have to *do* something in order to have worth, then you will have to establish your own self-worth through your actions. If you believe that people have innate worth simply because they are alive and unique, then your own self-worth will be justified by your simply being alive and unique.

The same applies to your definition of masculinity. The way you define masculine worth will influence how worthwhile you feel as a man. Our feelings of masculinity or femininity are right at the core of our self-concept. How successful we feel as men or women determines how worthy we feel as people. If you have a very narrow set of criteria for masculinity, then you will have a very restricted number of standards for masculine self-worth. If you have a broader set of criteria for masculinity, you will have a larger number of resources with which to define masculine self-worth. Below are several different definitions of the meaning of masculinity.

The Machismo Definition

The machismo definition advocates masculinity at its most primitive level. Central to the machismo definition are the following:

Unrestrained sexual conquest. According to this approach, women are looked upon as sexual trophies to be conquered and placed on the mantel. Among the poverty-stricken, having children (often by several different women) may also be a part of the definition. Manhood is defined in large part by sexual activity. Often men who follow this definition will be found in locker rooms or bars describing their latest "conquest."

Triumph over others. Men who take a machismo approach to life get great satisfaction through gaining victories over other men. This tendency was what Christ was addressing when He told His disciples, " 'You know that those who are regarded as rulers of the Gentiles lord it over them, and their high officials exercise authority over them. Not so with you. Instead, whoever wants to become great among you must be your servant, and whoever wants to be first must be slave of all' " (Mark 10:42–44 NIV).

Fighting. According to the machismo definition, fighting is a central criterion of masculinity. Those who can't or won't fight don't deserve the title "man." In fact, periodic brawls may be necessary in order to establish that one is, in fact, a man.

Swaggering. Men enmeshed in the machismo philosophy adopt a characteristic style of relating to others. It involves a swaggering, strutting, boastful demeanor that probably finds its closest nonhuman analogue in the peacock. Perhaps the best modern example of machismo swaggering is found in the boxing ring. Since the time Muhammad Ali became heavyweight champion of the world, it has become fashionable for boxing opponents to confront each other with a repertoire of hostile stares and intimidating gestures before a bout. In team sports, this is not the route to go because it often simply energizes the other team to try harder. But in individual sports, the aim is breaking your opponent's spirit before the action begins.

The machismo definition is most commonly found among adolescents and some subgroups of young homosexuals. The older you get, the less effective machismo swaggering becomes.

While the machismo definition of masculinity is certainly less than desirable for adolescents, its adoption by older men can have devastating effects upon a culture. It involves "masculinity" for its own sake. Courage, aggressiveness, and sexual behavior are not tied to a higher purpose.

Anthropologist Oscar Lewis wrote a book several years ago concerning the culture of poverty.[1] It has become a classic because it identified similarities in conditions of poverty across a variety of cultures. Dr. Lewis found that the poverty-stricken in different cultures showed the same patterns of behavior. One of those patterns was a strongly machismo philosophy among the men.

To what extent this machismo pattern *causes* poverty or *results* from the insecurity bred by proverty is unclear. But it seems likely that men who devote their time and energy to finding as large a pool of sexual partners as possible, who spend hours and hours with "the boys" swapping stories and playing games, and who enjoy fighting and brawling are not likely to have much energy or time left over to live a productive life. That's the major problem with machismo: it wastes masculine energy.

But another problem is that it can ruin a marriage. I

had a friend in high school who fully adopted the machismo definition of masculinity. Lloyd was the school bully. He picked on anyone and everyone, no matter what their size or strength. He was extremely aggressive and showed a tremendous amount of courage. He fought anyone who challenged him at the drop of a hat. Sometimes, too, he fought just for the fun of it. One night Lloyd and a friend of his were walking down the street when some less-than-macho schoolmates stopped to offer them a ride. They cheerfully accepted the ride; but in less than five minutes Lloyd and his companion had each chosen one of their schoolmates to beat up. With no warning, they leaned toward the front seat and started hitting the other two boys as hard as they could. The driver slammed on his brakes, and he and his companion fled from the car.

At an early age Lloyd started dating Janice, a gentle, easygoing girl. They went together for a long time, but finally Janice decided she wanted to date other boys. This dealt a crushing blow to Lloyd's ego: what could someone else possibly offer Janice that he wasn't already giving her? He pressured her to get married, and she eventually agreed.

Unfortunately Lloyd saw marriage as a means of insuring Janice's loyalty to him while placing no restrictions on his behavior. The first year or two, Lloyd didn't act like he was married at all. He continued to go out with his single friends, fighting and picking up girls. Even the birth of his first child didn't settle him down.

Lloyd's actions at home weren't much better, either. He criticized and belittled his wife at every opportunity. It didn't matter to him how he hurt or embarrassed her. I remember seeing the two of them at our high school reunion. Janice was catching up on all the news with several former girlfriends, and Lloyd walked over to join them. "You're having a ball gossiping, aren't you?" he commented to Janice. "You couldn't make it through the day unless you spread a little dirt about someone else."

Despite his ill-treatment of his wife and children, Lloyd never worried about his family's loyalty to him. "After all," he thought, "where would they find another *real man* like me?" One day, though, he came home from work and found that his wife had left with the kids, never to return. His macho approach to life had destroyed his family and their love for him.

Another problem with the machismo definition is that it can breed "strong, silent types" who don't share or communicate with their women. By not communicating, they don't grow, since talking is an important part of changing. Also, by not communicating, they fail to meet their wives' need for companionship, making their marriages less satisfying. And finally, by not communicating, they bottle things up inside, often ruining their own health.

Walt grew up in a cold, regimented family. Each member had assigned duties and roles, and the family operated like an efficient little army. Walt learned to organize to perfection, but unfortunately never learned to express his emotions—not warmth, affection, empathy; not fear, insecurity, or a need for support. He went through childhood and adolescence taking care of his own psychological needs as best he could, never reaching out to others.

Socially Walt was a lot of fun to be with. He told lively stories and had a quick wit. Women found him very attractive, so he had no problem finding a lovely wife, Anna. Anna thoroughly enjoyed their courtship and looked forward to a life spent with Walt. But once they married, things began to change in their relationship. As Anna strived for the intimacy she hoped for in marriage, as she began to share her deepest feelings with Walt, she noticed it made him strangely uncomfortable. And if she tried to get him to communicate his feelings with her, he would become hostile and refuse to talk. This kind of sharing, he felt, was not appropriate for a man.

Small problems began to turn into major crises because Walt wouldn't communicate with Anna. When Walt was growing up, his mother always had dinner on the table at six P.M. sharp. He expected the same from Anna. But instead of sitting down and explaining his desires to her, Walt just criticized Anna for always being late with meals. And if his criticism hurt her and she tried to discuss it with him, Walt would clam up. Anna became more and more frustrated and unhappy in her marriage because, although she knew that Walt loved her, she couldn't foresee any change in their relationship. "After all," she thought, "how can we work out our problems if we can't even discuss them?"

Walt, in turn, felt unhappy with Anna's demands for communication. He just wanted to ignore their problems and hope they would magically disappear. That is what his childhood family had always done. In fact, in all his growing-up years he had witnessed only two very brief and insignificant confrontations between his parents. Of course, he also remembered the underlying tension that dominated the household.

Finally Walt's inner turmoil, which he refused to let

out verbally, expressed itself as a physical symptom. He developed stomach ulcers and had to restrict his diet greatly for some time. Still he would not communicate and has not learned to do so to this day.

It's not hard to see that the machismo definition of masculinity is one of the most undesirable and dead-end standards that men can go by. For that reason, it has been unpopular for a number of years. Women just aren't impressed with it anymore, if they really ever were.

Machismo is an extreme definition of masculinity. And while very few people today would support this extreme interpretation of masculine behavior, we have to be careful not to go to the other extreme and reject male traits altogether. Physical courage, competitiveness, and aggressiveness all have their place, especially if they are harnessed to a higher goal or purpose. Properly channeled, they are valuable attributes, both necessary and desirable in society.

Unfortunately, some people in their haste to reject the fanaticism of machismo have also dismissed as worthless some uniquely masculine strengths. They have thrown up the red flag of male chauvinism and have seen expressions of the male nature simply as ways to compensate for insecurity.

Increasingly we are seeing masculine traits of initiative, courtesy, and courage derided by women who seem almost afraid of men and their characteristics. Every month or so Ann Landers prints a letter from a disgruntled gentleman who has nearly gotten his face slapped because he offered his seat to a woman on a bus. He's in real trouble, too, if he opens the car door for his date: "Is he trying to say she's too weak to open her own door?!"

This new militant independence on the part of some women can reach ridiculous proportions. I read recently about a man, Norm, who took his very attractive date to a restaurant. While they were eating dessert, a stranger came up to the date and made a blatant pass at her. Norm jumped to his feet and told the stranger to "get lost." To Norm's amazement, his date began giving him a tongue-lashing: "Listen, Norm," she said, "I'm perfectly able to take care of myself, and I don't appreciate your meddling in my affairs. From now on please mind your own business!" Norm stood there in shock as she folded her napkin, placed it on the table, and marched out of the restaurant.

When women fail to esteem masculine traits and their pursuant actions, they can come up with some pretty outlandish motives for male behavior. Shortly after a period of national emergency when President Nixon placed American military troops on alert, a leading feminist appeared on a nationally televised talk show. The conversation turned to the recent crisis, and the feminist, asked to give her interpretation of the event, stated that the president's actions demonstrated his sexual insecurity. He put the troops on alert, she theorized, to display his aggressiveness and cover up his feelings of sexual inadequacy.

The Traditional Definition

The traditional approach to masculinity is the most common definition across all cultures. It will vary somewhat from one culture to the next, but it seems to be the norm in most cultures. The traditional definition generally includes the following:

The man as provider. Traditionally, men have been given

the major role of providing for their families. How well a man fills that role determines, in part at least, his status as a man.

In biblical times Abraham held the respect of surrounding nations as well as his own family, in part because of his noble and generous character, but also because of his vast holdings. He had cattle, sheep, silver, gold, and numerous servants with which to support his family, thus earning him a place of high status.

Things aren't a lot different today. Men still gain or lose prestige depending on how well they provide for their families. I remember an incident in one of my graduate classes several years ago. Wilson, a young man in the class, was working toward a Ph.D. in counseling. He was quiet, sharing very little of his personal life with the other students; but everyone assumed he was getting an advanced degree to support his family better.

One day, however, Wilson told the class how his wife, the evening before, had been reading a medical journal while preparing dinner. As his narrative continued, everyone realized that his wife was a physician and that she was supporting him. I noticed that most of the students, especially the women, looked surprised at first and then subtly began to check around the room to see if others had come to the same conclusion. From that day on I noticed a change in the students' interactions with Wilson. They seemed to feel somewhat uncomfortable around him, having trouble knowing exactly how to relate to him and his situation. His status in the class dropped considerably; although he himself had not changed at all, the students' perceptions of him were altered when they discovered that he was not fulfilling the traditional role of provider.

Quite a few variants of the provider role exist. In some cultures a rigid division of labor is upheld. Only men provide. In most cultures, however, women share this responsibility as well, but the major part of the providing is done by men. For reasons given in previous chapters, men and women get along much better, and marriages are happier, when the man does the major share of supporting the family.

Nothing in the traditional definition would dictate that women should not provide at all (although a minority of men feel threatened by even slight female economic contributions) as long as men do more. Both the Old and New Testaments contain accounts of women who helped support the family or managed family affairs. First Samuel tells of Abigail, an extremely poised and intelligent woman, who had to oversee her husband's entire estate because he lived in a constant state of drunkenness. The Book of Ruth relates how the young widow Ruth joined a group of self-supporting women to glean the fields of Boaz so that she and her mother-in-law would have food to eat. In the New Testament we learn about Lydia and Priscilla, two career women. While Lydia probably had to support herself by selling purple dye after her husband's death, Priscilla worked as a tentmaker right alongside her husband and the apostle Paul.

But the traditional approach does require that men provide in order to feel good about themselves as men. Men who follow this approach (and that would include most men) would base their self-worth on whether they provide successfully for the family and, sometimes, on how much they provide.

Several years ago a nationally known football star got

in to a contract dispute with the owner of his franchise. It seems he had played such inspired football that he had fired up his whole team. Under his leadership, a disgruntled and frustrated group of men had come together to form a championship unit. But the player's new salary demands were considered unreasonable by the management, so they refused to sign his contract. The player decided to sit out the preseason rather than reduce his bid. It was quite a gamble to take. He risked alienating the other players, not to mention his fans, who would probably consider him greedy.

Eventually the player signed the contract for the amount he originally requested, and several reporters asked him the same question. "Considering the harm your absence has done the team, and in view of your fans' disenchantment with you, was it really worth it?" Every time this question was put to him the player had the same reply. "I feel sure that it was worth all the hassle and hard feelings because now I *know* that my family has financial security." This player was willing to put his career and reputation on the line in order to provide well for his family. His self-worth was firmly grounded, not in his football achievements alone, but also in the knowledge that he was taking care of every need his wife and children might have.

The problem occurs when a man loses his provider role through no fault of his own—by being laid off or crippled, for example. Are we saying that a man's self-worth is shot when he's not providing? As I'll discuss further later on, a great danger is inherent in basing your self-worth *exclusively* on one narrow criterion.

The man as leader. In addition to providing for the family, the traditional definition emphasizes the man's leadership role in the home. Men are expected to have the major role in making decisions about the family—to set its standard of living, to be consulted about all important family issues, and to serve in the top position in a hierarchy of authority that goes from father to mother to children.

Of course, the concept of leader is much vaguer than the concept of provider. Although the husband may be recognized as the official head of the household, most homes don't revolve around the pattern of husband telling the wife what to do and the wife simply doing it. In reality the question of the man's leadership position is often decided in the smaller issues of life. A husband might comment that he really likes his wife to wear her dresses a certain length. She can choose to ignore his remark and wear her clothes however she wants to, or she can try to accommodate his desires out of love and respect for him. He might ask that she have the car filled up with gas every Friday so the family will be ready for any unplanned excursions. Then she can either make that one of her top priority items or she can let it slide until everything else is done.

Our concept of the role of leader is changing in the general culture, so naturally our concept of what leadership means in the family is changing also. Just as we are moving toward a more humanistic, democratic form of leadership in social organizations, we are also moving in the same direction in our parental leadership roles. Husbands and wives discuss issues before making decisions, and they negotiate (at least in well-functioning homes). It's probably accurate to say that the traditional definition of masculinity sees male leadership as a potential attribute, not as a rigid pattern that husband-wife interactions must always follow.

But given these qualifications, men do tend to base

their self-worth on the extent to which they feel competent as leaders in the home. One way to evaluate this vague concept of leadership is to ask, "Who is the more dominant partner in the family?" Studies indicate that when the wife is the more dominant partner, both husband and wife are more dissatisfied with the marriage than when the husband is more dominant.[2] The same relationship has been demonstrated between decision-making and marital happiness: the more decisions wives are forced to make because their husbands shun their responsibilities in that area, the unhappier both spouses are.

My wife attended a women's Bible class several years ago in which they studied the subject of leadership in the home. Most of the women really enjoyed the topic. One woman, however, grew more and more dissatisfied with the lessons as the weeks went on. She mainly discussed her complaints outside the group itself, but one day someone asked her directly during class why she wanted to discontinue the study of leadership and change to another, more "worthwhile" topic. "Well," she told the ladies, "this subject just isn't relevant in my life. My husband refuses to take the leadership role, and nothing I do will change his mind. He refuses to make any major decisions, and I'm left with the total responsibility. And who gets the blame if anything goes wrong? Of course, it's me!" This woman was almost in tears as she talked. The lack of male leadership in her home placed an unnecessary burden of responsibility on her shoulders. And sadly, this situation didn't make life any easier for her husband either.

Division of labor. According to the traditional approach to masculinity, each sex has something unique to contribute to a marriage or family—something that the other sex can't as easily offer. Those uniquely different contributions are embodied in a set of sexual roles that determine activities considered appropriate for one sex or the other. Traditional men evaluate their self-worth according to how effectively they fulfill their sexual role.

A man may find great enjoyment and satisfaction doing things that aren't considered masculine in the traditional sense. A friend of mine who has a highly successful law practice loves to bake bread. He spends almost every other weekend concocting some new bread recipe, and he has won several baking contests. But this activity is a creative outlet for him. It does not give him the same feelings of self-worth and achievement that his career does.

Generally the roles that men see as masculine are as follows: work at a job; keep the yard up (as opposed to the inside of the house); do all the home repairs; keep the cars and all machinery running.

The pattern of roles usually varies somewhat from one home to another. But these are the typical sex roles for men. And of the ones mentioned above, the first, working at a job, is the crucial one for most men.

As mentioned in earlier chapters, these role divisions seem most compatible with our sexual natures and, hence, seem to work better than other patterns. One of the problems with the traditional approach, though, is that in the past we've underestimated the importance of the father in the home. Instead of emphasizing the father's unique contribution to the children's development, we've acted as if the father's importance in the home ends with his paycheck, and the mother is the only parent who needs to spend time with the children.

This has been an extremely damaging philosophy for both children and fathers. As I mentioned earlier, the father has a unique influence on the children's development in the areas of psychological adjustment, leadership behavior, social skills, academic performance, and occupational success, among others. Children who grow up without effective fathers suffer in all these areas.

But fathers suffer as well in that they are cut off from an important source of self-worth—their success as fathers. By placing all their emphasis upon occupational success, men neglect another potentially satisfying area. Many a man has pursued the goal of occupational success so single-mindedly that he neglects his family; then when he has achieved all he wants, he begins to yearn for his children, but they are not there. They've become accustomed to living their lives without him. That's the point where these men usually cease to gain a feeling of self-worth from their jobs, and life in general becomes less meaningful for them.

So the traditional definition of masculinity may be undergoing a slight change. Instead of emphasizing the father's unique contribution outside the sphere of parenting, it has begun to recognize the unique contribution of the father as a parent.

This is a welcome change. In the past the major weakness of the traditional definition has been its neglect of fathering.

But the traditional pattern does have several advantages. One, as mentioned above, is that it is compatible with our sexual natures. Another is that practically all marriages drift into the traditional pattern within five years of marriage even if they began as equalitarian ones. Spouses are happier, in general, with some variation of the traditional pattern.

The Androgyny Definition

Androgyny is a very popular current topic in the behavioral sciences. The word is a synthesis of masculine and feminine roots: *andros*, meaning male, and *gyne*, meaning female. The word "androgyny" refers to a combination of masculine and feminine attributes, usually in one person.

Androgyny has become more than a word, though. It is now a philosophy of the ideal man or woman.

For years, the field of psychology followed the Eriksonian model of masculinity and femininity. That is, the healthy male was one who possessed a large degree of "masculine" traits and who felt secure in his own masculinity. The healthy female likewise had "feminine" attributes and was secure in her own femininity. Neither sex had many behaviors or traits normally associated with the other, and masculinity/femininity were seen as polar opposites on a single continuum, as follows:

Masculinity _____Femininity

Where one scored on this continuum determined how masculine or feminine one was.

In the early 1970s, a social psychologist named Sandra Bem[3] offered a challenge to the Eriksonian model. If masculinity and femininity are on opposite ends of a continuum, she reasoned, that means if you're high on one, you're automatically low on the other. Why couldn't you be high on *both* masculinity and femininity? In other words, why couldn't you possess both masculine and feminine attributes?

Bem eventually put together a test that consisted of separate masculine and feminine scales, as follows:

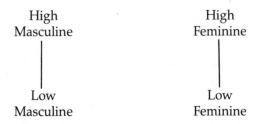

High Masculine	High Feminine
Low Masculine	Low Feminine

According to this approach, the person who scores high on both the masculine and feminine scales is "androgynous" (i.e., has both masculine and feminine traits). If you score low on masculine and high on feminine, you are "feminine-typed" (possess mainly feminine traits); and if you score high on masculine and low on feminine, you are "masculine-typed" (possess mainly masculine traits). People who score low on both scales, and who thus possess few traits, either masculine or feminine, are called "undifferentiated." (As we'll see later, these people are the worst off of the four categories.)

Bem's main idea was that androgynous people would be the emotionally and psychologically healthiest of the four groups. Androgynous people would combine the masculine traits of aggressiveness, independence, and ambition with the feminine attributes of tenderness, sensitivity, and nurturance. Thus, they would be able to function well in a variety of situations and would have higher self-esteem and better social relationships.

This new model is in direct opposition to the old Eriksonian approach, which says "be masculine if you're male and feminine if you're female." Men who use the androgynous definition would define their self-worth according to the number of masculine *and* feminine attributes they possess. Thus the androgynous model complicates things; not only do you have to establish yourself as a man, at the same time you also have to establish your feminine side.

But people who propose an androgynous model would say that the feminine traits were there within you all along: it is the *culture* that arbitrarily separates us into masculine or feminine categories and thus prevents us from developing the full range of our own personalities. That assertion is one of the weaknesses of the androgyny philosophy. As we discussed earlier, some sex differences in personality attributes are definitely biologically-based. The sexes don't start out equal only to have the culture suppress their opposite sex characteristics.

But even with this weakness in mind, the androgyny approach has a point. Neither sex can afford to cut themselves off completely from the attributes associated with the other sex. Some men no doubt define their masculinity in terms of the absence of feminine traits in their personality. Anything that smacks of the feminine is to be shunned. Thus they cut themselves off from the tender emotions, the gentle behaviors.

Several years ago I met Bill, a man who seemed committed to becoming as totally masculine as possible. His father had died when Bill was a small boy, and Bill had grown up in a household totally dominated by women. They dressed him in fancy clothes and always kept his hair perfectly in place. They taught him all the rules of etiquette and expected him to fit right in their feminine world. But Bill rebelled and began a pursuit of masculinity that would last a lifetime. He quickly learned to fight and defend himself. He worked out with weights and developed a massive physique. In later years his aggressive quest for success in the business world knew no bounds. At the same time, Bill spurned anything that reminded him of his childhood encounters with femininity. He refused to do any work around the house—"That's a woman's job," he'd tell his wife. He had few interactions with his children. He avoided any display of tender emotions like the plague. Bill was a man's man, but he missed many life-enhancing experiences along the way.

No man should define his masculinity in such a negative manner—as the absence of feminine traits. Masculinity should be seen as a more positive experience. Where a man is truly secure in his own masculinity, he can allow some of those attributes that are usually called feminine to reveal themselves. In fact, those "feminine" traits help determine how the masculine ones are expressed.

But the key here is that men must first be secure in their masculinity before they feel comfortable expressing feminine traits. And that is one of the weaknesses of androgyny: it doesn't really provide a special way for men to develop a secure masculinity. It seems to be saying that we're all the same, and we should all attempt to equalize our goals, contributions, and behaviors. That is anathema to the majority of men, who typically need a special set of goals and roles in order to feel secure. By carrying a good idea to such an extreme, the androgyny definition undercuts its own effectiveness.

For example, proponents of androgyny usually advocate that we raise our children without any reference to what's masculine or feminine. In other words, we don't differentiate between masculine and feminine, and we actively encourage both sexes to perform the behaviors associated with the opposite sex. That plan is supposed to produce androgynous adults.

But another possibility is that rather than producing androgynous adults, it might create undifferentiated ones (remember, undifferentiated people are those who score low on both masculine and feminine scales). Maybe by failing to differentiate between masculine and feminine, we could fail to give our boys and girls anyone to identify with, thus further confusing their sexual identities.

Other problems exist for the androgyny definition. The contention has always been that androgynous people would be better adjusted than sex-typed ones. But research has been inconsistent. Androgynous individuals, for example, have no higher self-esteem than masculine-typed persons. And one study found that rapists are much more androgynous than the normal population. These results are not likely to establish any great confidence in or enthusiasm for the philosophy of androgyny.

One of the findings that shows up in androgyny research is the importance of masculinity. Researchers have found that those people who score highest on self-esteem and occupational performance scales possess predominantly masculine, not androgynous, traits. This probably results from cultural values. We've so upheld the masculine and downplayed the feminine that masculine attributes have become important for both sexes. In a less competitive, less individualistic culture, masculinity might not be so crucial. But in this society, if you want to feel good about yourself and be effective at work, you'd better develop as many masculine attributes as possible.

This has been a very discouraging trend, and I've written about it in other books. We've made it very hard for women to develop a sense of self-esteem within their own feminine natures by our emphasis upon masculine traits and goals. And as a culture we've cut ourselves off from the feminine attributes just as some men do.

But given these unfortunate results, the androgynous definition, swallowed whole, would seem to offer little comfort to most men. It simply doesn't help them with their most nagging task—to first develop a secure masculine identity.

What can we conclude about the androgyny philosophy? As mentioned earlier, its major contribution is its recognition that both sexes can profit to a certain extent from having some of the attributes associated with the other sex. Men who cut themselves off from tenderness, sharing, and gentleness also cut themselves off from one of the most important experiences of life—an intimate relationship with a woman. Only so much satisfaction can be enjoyed in the world of men. Most men, in order to feel fully masculine, need a close relationship with a woman, for we define masculinity in large part by its relationship to femininity. Most women, in order to feel good about their men, need to see those attributes of tenderness and gentleness displayed at least every now and then.

The Achievement-Productivity Definition

For most men, jobs are a crucial part of their feelings of masculine security. And when they lose their jobs, men become poorer husbands, fathers, and lovers. The statistics on unemployment bear this out. Men who lose their jobs experience an increase in child abuse, spouse abuse, alcoholism, mental disorders, divorce, and suicide.

In part, a job is important to a man because it provides that external role he needs to affirm his own masculinity. Women might want a job. They may experience a need for a job. But it's not the same as with men. A woman can lose her job without any of the pathological results listed above. A woman has something to fall back on.

But jobs are important to masculine security for another reason: they connect a man to a woman. Women are attracted to men who are producing or achieving. The more a man has achieved, the more attractive women will find him. It's fascinating to attend a school reunion and discover how your friends and acquaintances have changed. And it's especially interesting to watch the women's (and men's) reactions to the news that a shy bookworm from high school has become a successful banker or politician. The girls who wouldn't give him a second glance in their teens become vitally interested in every detail of his life, all because of his achievements.

Also, men need a channel for their sexual and aggressive energies. Jobs and achievements provide such a channel. In the ghetto, jobs are lacking, so masculine energy is channeled into drugs, crime, violence, gang warfare, and often suicide. Those problems afflict men much more often than women, even though women are subject to the same scourges of unemployment and meaninglessness that men have to face. But the women don't succumb as often. Their identities as women, and

[197]

their access to men, aren't on the line through their achievements.

Strong voices in our culture attempt to deny this. We hear that a man's special need for a meaningful job is completely a product of our own sexist culture (despite Margaret Mead's observation that it occurs in *all* cultures). But it has been my observation that most of the people who decry the assertion that jobs and achievements are more important for men than women *still live lives that prove the assertion.*

Jobs and achievements are a crucial cornerstone in the male ego structure. It's easy to build a philosophy of masculinity based upon productive contributions and achievements. So many masculine rewards result from working and achieving that men can easily come to define themselves and their masculinity completely in terms of their achievements.

But this definition of masculinity has some severe limitations and disadvantages associated with it. What about the man who loses his job? His company lays off workers for economic reasons and he finds himself unemployed—perhaps for several years. Is he entitled to no feeling of masculine self-worth during this period in his life?

Or what about the man who is paralyzed in an accident and loses his job? Does he also lose his self-worth?

Often the talents and drive that lead to achievement simply decline with age. As men lose their ability to achieve, do they also lose their sense of self-worth? That is what happened to Ernest Hemingway. He lost some of his writing skills during his older years. As he watched his skills decline, his feelings of worth as a man also declined until he finally ended his life.

Usually it doesn't take something as drastic as the loss of a job or the decline of skills to cause a man to question his self-worth. Often just a setback at work can bring about real ego problems for a man who has adopted the productivity definition of masculinity. I counseled recently with a man who was experiencing depression and despair because of a crisis at his office. It seems that he had made an unpopular decision affecting a number of his employees; the workers, rather than keeping their dissatisfaction to themselves, had united in opposition to the man and his authority over them. At the height of emotion, they had called for his resignation or dismissal.

When my client learned of the widespread dissension he had caused, he withdrew from contact with everyone—his employees, his friends, his family. He felt crushed and betrayed; he had not intended to hurt or anger anyone by his decision, but suddenly he felt that everyone was making a villain out of him, using him as a scapegoat for all their anger and frustration. When I talked with my client about his feelings of self-worth, he said he had none at all. His good relationship with his family, his contributions to his church and the community, his wide circle of friends no longer gave him self-esteem. Because things had gone badly at work, he felt his whole life was a failure.

So, although jobs and achievements are a realistic part of masculinity, the achievement definition can easily expand until it determines too much of a man's self-worth. Men who define themselves exclusively by their jobs and achievements are taking a very vulnerable stance in today's economy. Even if they keep their jobs and achieve great things, they still err by making their work all-important. Men have too much to contribute in other areas to make the mistake of defining themselves narrowly. Marriage, family, and children should be a part of the male sense of self-worth.

The Christian Definition

The Christian definition emphasizes that man is made in the image of God and that he is designed primarily to have fellowship with his Creator. This definition of masculinity provides men with masculine goals and a source of masculine self-worth that go beyond immediate desires and earthly concerns. In other words, it diverts attention from fleshly lusts and turns them toward higher, more noble pursuits. As a result, this definition is diametrically opposed to the machismo definition of masculinity.

The Christian definition has the advantage of channeling all the masculine drives and needs into higher aspirations. According to this definition, for example, aggressiveness is not ideally channeled into fighting. The purpose of the aggressive drive is to enable us to show effective leadership behavior, to use our talents efficiently (without aggressiveness our talents would lie dormant), to display initiative, and to exercise "dominion over the earth."

In a similar manner, the Christian definition views sex as a gift from God, to be channeled and enjoyed within the bounds of marriage. It's a drive that ideally becomes attached to child-bearing, child-rearing, husbanding, and fathering.

The Christian definition of self-worth takes a similar approach to all drives. Our daily activities are harnessed to a higher purpose—to glorify God. This gives a meaning to what we do and is above the concept of masculinity.

But the Christian definition of self-worth goes far beyond the act of channeling human drives. Our self-worth is permanently established by God's love for us. The Christian message is that God loves us so much that He died for us. We are so important to Him that He has employed all of His limitless resources to give us continued fellowship with Him. And He continues to minister to us today. That love and that intervention verify our worth as men and women.

The Christian definition of self-worth is based upon God's love for humanity. All people are important to God. But God doesn't lump them together; rather, he recognizes each person's individuality and tailors His interventions for the individual. According to this definition, God has a plan for each life. The person who is willing to submit his life to God's plan will find his talents utilized productively and his life given an aim and purpose.

In a sense, the Christian definition of self-worth encompasses all the other definitions (except for the machismo). It ties masculine drives to the family, like the traditional definition; it offers some "feminine" attributes (such as love and gentleness) to men, thus rounding out their natures, like the androgynous definition; and it gives men an opportunity to achieve by tying their talents to God's plan, like the achievement definition.

TEN

Self-esteem and Ego-deflating Beliefs

After self-worth, self-esteem is probably the most important part of the ego. In fact, our self-esteem is based in part on the way we define our own worth. As mentioned in the last chapter, how we feel about ourselves depends to some extent on how we assign worth to human beings. If we place a high value on accomplishments, for example, then in order to have solid self-worth, we had better have some solid accomplishments (or we had better change our values).

Self-esteem is emotional, whereas self-worth is more intellectual. Thus self-esteem is the way we feel about ourselves. It is the experience we're most aware of on a day-to-day basis. The way we think about ourselves in general doesn't carry quite the same weight as the way we feel about ourselves at any given moment. A man may know rationally that he is intelligent (IQ scores measure that) and talented (his teachers and friends have always said he is), but he may feel like a failure if he isn't doing well in his job.

This is a complex issue that I'll return to later. Suffice it to say that our self-esteem depends on our definitions of self-worth. But it depends on more than that, as well.

The Experience of Self-esteem

Since self-esteem is in part an emotional experience, we'd expect it to rise and fall with the emotions. To some extent this is true. Manic-depressives, people who experience strong swings in mood from low to high, also undergo corresponding swings in self-esteem. When they're low, they feel worthless and valueless; when their mood swings back up, their self-esteem also rises—sometimes to the point where they become grandiose in their thinking.

I had a student in graduate school who suffered from strong mood swings. He did excellent work, but I could always tell what part of the cycle he was in. On his manic days, he participated actively in class discussions, presenting creative ideas with enthusiasm and energy. He possessed great confidence in his ability to carry through on class projects, and he inspired the other students to greater achievements. On his down days, however, he would sit in the back of the room, in as inconspicuous a place as possible. He volunteered nothing in the class discussions, speaking only if I asked him a direct question. He did well on tests during all parts of his mood cycle; but when he was down, he felt as though he had failed the test completely.

This is an example of swings in self-esteem because of internal factors. But self-esteem also fluctuates because of external factors. Rejections, failures, successes, and other circumstances cause our self-esteem to fluctuate likewise.

Not everyone reacts to positive and negative events with the same degree of change in self-esteem. Some people experience swings from high self-esteem when they are praised, loved, or successful to very low self-esteem when they are criticized, rejected, or unsuccessful.

These people are like cold-blooded animals. An animal with a cold-blooded nervous system, such as a frog or snake, does not have an internal regulator that keeps its body temperature at a constant level. The frog's body temperature will rise if the outside temperature rises, and it will drop if the outside temperature drops. Its body temperature is completely dependent on its surroundings.

Many people have the self-esteem equivalent of a cold-blooded nervous system. They feel good about themselves when things go well and bad about themselves when things go poorly. They lack a sense of inner ego strength independent of their immediate situation.

Mollie had this sort of intense reaction to other people's opinions. She grew up in a family where her parents controlled her behavior by giving or withholding love. If Mollie did everything just right, her parents treated her well, spent time talking with her, and gave her attention and affection. But if she did something that displeased them, rather than discussing it with her, they just ignored her, refused to talk to her, and wouldn't even look at her. So Mollie grew up very sensitive to other people's reactions. If people praised her performance at teaching, for example, her self-esteem shot up and she thought about all the successes she'd had instructing her students. But if she received criticism, it was just like sticking a pin into a balloon. All of Mollie's self-confidence vanished, and try as she might, she couldn't think of a single positive thing about her teaching career.

Most people are stronger than Mollie. They come down some when they fail, and they feel better when they succeed. But their self-esteem doesn't fluctuate wildly with changes in their circumstances. They have an inner strength that prevents them from being constantly threatened with the loss of self-esteem.

In this sense, they are like all warm-blooded animals. Human beings and other mammals are blessed with an internal regulator that maintains their body temperature at a relatively stable level within a wide range of outside temperatures. If the temperature is 110 degrees outside, our body temperature is still close to 98.6 degrees. If the outside temperature drops to 45 degrees, our body temperature doesn't come crashing down. People who have the warm-blooded equivalent of self-esteem show the same sort of internal stability despite environmental fluctuations. They can maintain a good feeling about themselves in the face of adversity and prosperity.

Christ, in my opinion, possessed the ultimate in warm-blooded self-esteem. He was never elated by success or flattery, and He was never crushed or discouraged by rejection and failure. In the hour when His name was spoken most enthusiastically, on the triumphant march to Jerusalem, His ego was not seduced by the accolades. Instead, He chose that time to weep over the soon-to-be desolate city and scattered people. Likewise, after having received ignominious rejection—in the form of insult, physical and psychological abuse, and finally death—at the hands of His own people, His first assignment to His disciples was to go back to Jerusalem to try to win back the rejectors. That took a very secure ego.

Some people seem to be able to maintain a strong ego in the face of mood swings or chance circumstances.

These people usually possess a source of internal strength or stability that allows them to maintain their self-esteem despite feeling low. What is it that contributes to their warm-blooded experience of self-esteem?

One contributor is the amount of love and acceptance they received during childhood, first and most importantly from the parents and second from the peer group. People who are given a healthy and consistent dose of love and acceptance develop the ability to love and accept themselves no matter what their immediate situation is like. Their self-esteem resists the influence of adversity, failure, and unpleasantness.

Recently I talked with a six-year-old boy who had just played in his first violin recital. He told me enthusiastically about how well he had done, how he had played a song without even having to learn it. His mother told me later that her son could play only three notes on his violin, but that he was convinced he had played two whole songs, just because he had heard the rest of the violinists in the group playing. (He played in a group of about forty, many of whom had taken lessons for years.) That little fellow had high self-esteem despite his limited knowledge and poor performance. He chose to think positively about himself.

But people who aren't given the love and acceptance they need for healthy ego development grow up very dependent on their environments. They look to other people—or to fame, power, and success—rather than to themselves, for the experience of self-esteem. Every minor insult or rejection becomes a devastating blow to their self-esteem. Achievements and accomplishments become the great test of self-worth. Lacking a strong ego within, they look outside for their happiness.

Self-esteem and Ego-deflating Beliefs

One common way that cold-blooded self-esteem types seek to establish their self-worth is through recognition. They aren't as interested in doing a job well as they are in receiving credit and praise for their accomplishments. My wife worked with a couple like this several years ago. Their main goal in life was to get in the limelight. Although they were less talented than some of their colleagues, they volunteered for every assignment that would give them recognition. They gave seminars and workshops, speeches and interviews. As long as they received acclaim, they felt good about themselves. But everyone soon discovered that although they had plenty of time to do the "up front" work, they never got around to doing anything behind the scenes; that sort of job just didn't bolster their egos.

Another strategy often used to bolster self-esteem is to seek approval from others. People who employ this technique are less sure of themselves, less confident than those who seek recognition. They don't hear a compliment or word of praise and then remain high until someone criticizes them; rather they constantly search for reassurance of their worth from others. One woman I counseled used a strange variation of this strategy. She would throw out a controversial statement like, "All the problems in our country would be solved if we just sent back the immigrants to their own countries"; then she would wait to see if people agreed with her (thereby establishing her self-esteem) or argued with her viewpoint (putting her down). This overall strategy of seeking the approval of others seems to be used predominantly by women. Most men value their independence too much to utilize it.

A third way that cold-blooded self-esteem types seek

ego strength is through accomplishments. This strategy is the male counterpart to women's search for acceptance and approval. The more achievements these men can get under their belts, the better they feel about themselves. Take Al, for example. He grew up more than a little unsure of his parents' love. They always seemed too busy for him and his interests. And when they spent time with him, they were very critical. So Al didn't have a lot of internal self-esteem. He felt as though he had to prove himself.

During his early twenties he changed jobs several times, always making a big gain in money and prestige. When he decided to stick with one company, he began making rapid advancement up the management ladder. With every promotion, he set a new and higher goal. He developed a strong and secure ego by his continual accomplishments, but he was never quite satisfied. He always strived for more.

Beliefs and Self-esteem

Although a secure and loving family background gives a person the best chance of internal self-esteem, he can also learn to be at peace with himself by adjusting his own set of beliefs about happiness and self-worth. An entire field of counseling and psychotherapy has sprung up, which is based upon the assumption that our deeply-held beliefs go a long way toward determining our psychological adjustment.

In a nutshell, this approach verifies what the Roman philosopher Marcus Aurelius said over two millennia ago: "A man is hurt, not so much by what happens, but by his *opinion* of what happens." In other words, our interpretations of events determine how we will feel about them; and our interpretations depend upon our beliefs.

Clinical psychologist Albert Ellis was one of the first psychologists to put this idea into scientific terms.[1] He proposed that when something happens (a person insults you), and you react emotionally to that event (you feel a loss of self-esteem), that event did not cause your emotional reaction. Rather, your beliefs about the event led to your emotional reaction.

To put it in concrete terms, if you hold the following belief—*I must be loved and approved of by every significant person in my life in order to love and approve of myself*—then when someone disapproves of or rejects you, your self-esteem will plummet. But, according to Dr. Ellis, your emotional reaction results from this irrational belief, not from the act of disapproval or rejection. Dr. Ellis would have the person who holds this self-esteem-depleting belief replace it with the following one: *It's nice to be loved and approved of. But it's better to love than to be loved.*

It has been my experience that women hold the irrational belief listed above much more often than men. Women frequently base their self-esteem on the love and approval they receive, while men more often rely on performance for their self-esteem. So, for men the following irrational belief would be a more likely cause of self-esteem problems: *I must be thoroughly competent, clever, successful, and achieving in everything I do in order to feel good about myself.*

In other words, the natural tendency that men have toward performing could be carried to such an extreme that self-esteem problems are inevitable. Whenever I hear words like *always, completely,* and *thoroughly* used in the context of achieving or performing, I perk up. Those words tell me that the person is setting himself up for pain and possible depression. This irrational belief should be replaced with the following one: *It is good to try to do well. But I need to accept myself as an imperfect creature, as are all human beings.*

Frank learned this lesson on his own, but it took him many years. Frank had a harsh and critical father who had a negative comment about everything Frank did, even his most outstanding achievements. The day Frank won the state track meet, his dad gave him some pointers on how he could have done better. So Frank grew up always "falling short." During his second year in college, he gave up trying altogether and almost dropped out of school. Fortunately, he had a teacher who recognized his potential and took a special interest in him. The teacher gave him the encouragement and acceptance he had always lacked at home, and slowly Frank learned to accept himself, too. He eventually felt satisfied with less than perfect performance, less than a 4.0 grade-point average. And at the same time, his self-esteem improved and his ego was strengthened.

Failures seem to be especially difficult for men to take. But the pain of past failures can be made worse by a belief system that allows bad experiences to continue to hurt us in the present. One such belief is, *Because something once strongly affected my life, it should continue to affect it indefinitely.*

All of us go through some bad experiences. Some people go through horrible experiences. Often it takes much time and energy before we heal. But if we keep telling ourselves "I failed in the past, so I will fail in the future," we prolong the agony and prevent our self-esteem from regenerating.

It seems to me that introverted people, with excellent long-term memories, are especially prone to being hurt by past mistakes and failures. They can visualize past events so graphically that they react emotionally as if the events just took place. Somehow they seem compelled to keep dredging up bad memories rather than letting them go. These people need to substitute the following healthy belief for the irrational one: *I should try to learn from my mistakes and painful experiences, but I should not be overly attached to or prejudiced by them.*

Failure to let go of the painful experiences from the past can cause real problems in the present. Roy came to see me because of this very problem. He had been unfaithful to his wife during the early years of their marriage. When she learned of the affair, his wife volunteered to divorce him so that he could marry his girlfriend. But Roy still loved his wife and asked her to take him back. He felt truly sorry for his part in the affair. He felt so sorry, in fact, that he carried the guilt for thirty years. "I'll never be able to make up for the hurt I caused my wife," he told himself. But he tried. He treated her like a queen and never objected to anything she said or did to him. By the time I began counseling him, his marriage was so lopsided that Roy now served as the passive recipient of his wife's verbal abuse.

Another belief that I often hear during counseling sessions is, *I should define myself in terms of my failures and weaknesses rather than in terms of my strengths and successes.* This negative belief strikes hard at the self-concept. I've never heard anyone articulate this belief directly. But when I ask them to describe themselves to me, some clients reveal a bias against themselves by dwelling on the mistakes and flaws. Often, they seem resistant when I ask them to describe their assets. Suddenly their memories fail them.

People usually adopt this belief when they are suffering from a recent failure or are in the throes of depression. If a businessman expands his inventory to include a new line of products, for example, and those products just sit on the shelf and don't sell, the businessman might conclude, "I just don't have a knack for picking out new products that will sell. I guess I should be satisfied with my business as it is and not try to expand it. In fact, I might do better in another line of work." But once he gets past the initial sense of failure, he usually remembers all of the positive things he has done for his company and adjusts his beliefs accordingly.

Sometimes we hear this define-myself-by-weaknesses belief propounded by members of the clergy. "We are all worms and degenerates in the sight of God," one minister asseverated recently. This statement is incompatible with the Christian definition of self-worth I described earlier, which says that God's love for human beings verifies their worth. It is also incompatible with the parts of the Christian message that suggest we focus on the positives. Philippians 4:8 says, ". . . whatever things are true, whatever things are noble, whatever things are just, whatever things are pure, whatever things are lovely, whatever things are of good report, if there is any virtue and if there is anything praiseworthy—meditate on these things."

A better belief system to guide us would be something like the following: *I have both strengths and weak-*

nesses, successes and failures. I will continue to develop and focus on my strengths while I attempt to control my weaknesses. I will learn from my successes and failures and then turn my attention toward new concerns.

An irrational belief that I often uncover among depressed persons with low self-esteem goes like this: *I must be perfect in order to feel good about myself.* Generally people who hold this belief do not realize it. They are often surprised when I point it out to them. This belief is usually acquired during childhood from parents who punish severely for mistakes but do not reward as intently for successes. The child seeks their approval by attempting to live an error-free, completely successful life. Since perfection is impossible, the person who holds this belief is doomed to a permanently low sense of self-esteem, no matter how well he functions.

Frequently, when I ask people who hold this belief to describe a successful experience or a strength they possess, they will be unable to gain any true satisfaction from the descriptions. "Why doesn't that make you feel good about yourself?" I will ask. "Because I'm not *completely* successful," they will answer.

This answer, or some variant of it, is a sure tipoff for perfectionism. "Either I'm completely successful, or else I'm a failure." "Either I'm totally happy, or I'm miserable." These people engage in dichotomous thinking. They can't see or enjoy moderate successes or mild happiness. That's unfortunate because moderate success and happiness is the norm for practically everyone. The major successes and the excruciating periods of happiness are so rare it isn't worth sitting on the edge of your seat in anticipation of them.

As I'll mention later, one way to ferret out these irrational beliefs is to argue them down whenever they pop up. But another way is to *act* against them. I usually tell perfectionists to "make one small mistake a day in your work on purpose. Watch for other people's reactions, and keep telling yourself that you are worthwhile in the face of this mistake." There's nothing like action to promote growth.

Sometimes self-esteem is affected by the beliefs we hold about happiness—who is responsible for it and how we go about achieving it. One of the surest ways to set yourself up for unhappiness and ego problems is to hold the following belief: *My unhappiness is caused by external events and is forced on me by outside circumstances and people.* I recently counseled a married couple for problems communicating with each other. The husband was an aggressive man who had really thrown himself into the courtship. The wife, despite some doubts about her suitor, was swept off her feet. One of the problems was her ambivalence about whether she really wanted to be married to this man.

"He's really good to me in many ways," she said, "but I'm just not sure I want to be married to him. I'm not really attracted to him physically. If I had it to do over again, I wouldn't marry him." Then after a long pause she looked at me and said, "I just wonder if I couldn't be happier with someone else. Do you think I could?"

Her problem, among several others, was that she looked to external circumstances for her happiness. Given a reasonably satisfying marriage, she was asking, "Could I be happier if I changed mates?"

That is a dangerous belief to hold—that happiness comes mainly from our environments. It crops up very often in counseling sessions with dissatisfied people. "If

I just had a new job, a different spouse, a more attractive home, or great achievement, *then* I would be happy." This belief makes people extremely dependent upon their surroundings. A healthier belief would be, *Much of my unhappiness is caused or sustained by the view I take of things rather than by the things themselves.*

Probably the most accurate statement about happiness is: *People are happiest when they are lost in a cause or project that's bigger than themselves.*

Sensitive men often have problems with nonproductive beliefs. They may make their reactions to rejection more severe by indoctrinating themselves with the following statements: *If I am rejected, it indicates that I am worthless and undesirable;* or *If I am rejected, it is a catastrophe.*

I've seen men become so pathologically fearful of rejection that they regulate their entire lives in a way that avoids even the most harmless rejection. This was what happened to Frank, the man I described in chapter six. He was so fearful of sexual rejection from his wife that he just refused to initiate sex with her. He had to sit around and wait until she approached him. I've seen other men cut themselves off from women altogether and from a healthy social life, too, in order to prevent the remotest possibility of a rejection. These are the men who, during counseling, are instructed to "go out and collect at least ten rejections" to demonstrate that they can be rejected and still live through it. (Often, these men come back and say something like, "I ended up getting six rejections and four phone numbers.")

For the man who has consistently been repeating to himself these negative beliefs about rejection, substituting one of the following statements would be a big step toward growth: *Being rejected is actually a positive experience because it suggests that my goals are high and I'm trying hard and taking chances;* or *Rejections won't hurt me any more than I allow them to;* or *No one can go through life and do anything without being rejected occasionally.*

Practically anyone who wishes to be a writer has to learn to endure the writer's bane—rejection slips. The *Orlando Sentinel*[2] recently reported on a local author who has been through the experience of rejection many times. W. B. Parks had three picture books published in 1983. Two of the books were rejected at least ten times before he found a publisher. Parks, a cartoonist, says that he collected over four hundred rejections from one magazine.

How does he handle the process of being rejected? "I just laugh," he said. "I send them five cartoons a week. It's sort of a game. That's the way you have to look at rejections. I play chess with a guy in Maine—just the way I send my cartoons in to *New Yorker.*"

Most of the above beliefs are found among both men and women. But some are peculiar to men.

One such belief involves unemployment. Men tend to fear the loss of their jobs about as much as the loss of their families. Social scientists have verified the negative impact that unemployment has upon men. Harvey Brenner, a professor of health services at Johns Hopkins University, recently found a link between the unemployment rate and various personal and social dysfunctions.[3] He found that a rise in the unemployment rate of just 1 percent, if sustained over a six-year period, is associated with a 4.1 percent increase in suicide, a 5.7 percent increase in homicides, and a 4.3 percent increase in first-time admissions to state mental hospitals.

Self-esteem and Ego-deflating Beliefs

In a recent series of interviews, community mental health directors reported a drastic increase in families seeking help for problems related to joblessness. One of the main symptoms has come to be labeled the "explosive father." He accounts for much of the child abuse and wife abuse associated with unemployment. But many other problems also rise with unemployment—severe quarrels, depression, suicide attempts, excessive alcohol use, insomnia, and fatigue.

I counseled a man who had nearly all of these symptoms of unemployment, even though he still had a job. Gary had thoroughly enjoyed his work until the recession hit and management started cutting back on his hours. At first he worked thirty hours a week, then twenty-five, then twenty. By the time he came to see me, he was working only fifteen hours a week with no hope of things getting better in the near future.

Gary complained of depression: "I just sit around all day, knowing that there are lots of things that need to be done. I could work in the yard or clean the garage or wax the car. But I just don't care anymore. The house could fall apart around me, and I probably still wouldn't have the motivation to get up and do something about it." He fought with his wife nearly every day; she not only had the entire responsibility for maintaining the home and caring for the children, but she also had to cope with Gary's low moods. It was just too much for her to take, and she would lash out at Gary, who welcomed the chance to unload his anger and frustration on her. If they weren't quarreling, Gary was telling his wife how he'd like to "end it all." Gary began drinking, too, even though he had been reared in a very religious home and had never before touched a drop of alcohol in his life, even during the teen years when peer pressure was so strong.

As mentioned earlier, men have a natural dependence on work roles in order to bolster their egos. Given the male susceptibility to psychological trauma following job loss, how is the unemployed man best able to cope?

One answer is to avoid making it worse than it is by indoctrinating yourself with negative statements. A man who believes, and continues to tell himself "I must have a job and provide for my family *all the time* or I'm worthless," is making a need more imperative than it actually is. A more positive and realistic statement would be, "It's bad that I lost my job, but it says little about my worth as a man," or "I will continue to feel like a worthwhile person in the face of this unfortunate event."

Most job losses are temporary. A large proportion of the unemployed get new jobs within a year or so. The task is to hold on and prevent the ego from being overly damaged until a new job can be found. One way to do that is to monitor those statements we make to ourselves, those interpretations we make of events, on a daily basis. Remember what Marcus Aurelius said: "A man is hurt not so much by what happens, but by his opinion of what happens."

One of the major issues that unemployed men face is how to structure their time. Unemployment takes away an important outlet for male aggressive energies. That energy is often turned inward on the family, accounting for the child and spouse abuse.

Unemployed men typically need contact with their male buddies in order to shore up their flagging sense of masculinity. Usually that contact is with other men at the bar or in sporting events. But *Guideposts* magazine[4] recently reported on a group of men who gathered together for a different purpose.

Robert Miller, a manager for a large communications corporation in New York, heard of several friends who were out of work; so he invited them to his home and introduced them to a novel experiment. First each man introduced himself and described his situation to the others. Then the men discussed their experiences in coping with unemployment. They found out that they had a lot in common. One man named Hugh summed up the feelings of all the men: "I like this sharing business, because when you're down and out you tend to focus on yourself and your own problems. Your fear isolates you, cuts you off. You begin to think you're the only guy in the whole world who's out of work." At the end of the meeting, each was assigned a prayer buddy—someone he'd pray for daily and who would pray for him for the next thirty days.

The group met each week to share results and to provide companionship, and each week the number of participants grew. Eventually twenty-one men became involved. And what were the results of this experiment?

(1) Chuck, who felt bogged down and bored with his job, received several good job offers.

(2) George, an unemployed executive, found a position in Washington, D.C., and relocated his family. A year later he and his family were still happy with their new home and his new job.

(3) Jack, who had been forced into early retirement, opened up his own frame shop and is currently doing a thriving business.

(4) John, who had lost his job because of a back ailment, was healed and began his own business.

(5) Out of the twenty-one participants in the experi-

ment, eighteen had found jobs by the time Mr. Miller wrote his article.

This action met several needs: the need for masculine associations, the need to use aggressive energies productively (in prayer), and the need for help from a power outside oneself—God. (Unemployed men often feel there's no one in power who is really concerned with their problems.) And apparently God honored the requests of those men by providing them with jobs.

Sometimes this process of talking to ourselves, of telling ourselves positive things about bad situations and refusing to tell ourselves the negative is one of the few resources we have in trying to maintain secure egos. Our interpretations of events, rather than the events themselves, generally determine how secure and strong we feel.

ELEVEN

Ego Stages in a Man's Life

"He's just going through a stage!"

How often have we heard that from parents or, if we happen to be parents, said it ourselves? We easily recognize the existence of "stages" in the human life cycle. These stages are times when some change of behavior occurs or some critical event takes place that has the power to affect a person's life years later.

In fact, an entire field of psychology is devoted to identifying these stages of human development. One observation has been made about stages, at least in the popular press. Women's lives, it seems, are more sharply segmented by stages than men's lives. Menarche very concretely separates a developing woman from her own childhood. Marriage and the birth of children bring about greater changes in the lives of women than of men. And menopause is a more intense biological and psychological experience for women than for men. (In fact, there doesn't seem to be a biological male menopause.)

But men have their stages, too. Some of the events and changes they face have a strong influence on men's egos. For this reason, I've referred to these as "ego stages." Rather than dividing the male life cycle up into the usual categories (infancy, early childhood, middle childhood, etc.), I prefer to focus on those events that subtly or not-so-subtly mold a man's ego.

What's in a Name?

The first event that subtly molds a man's ego throughout his life takes place very early in life, some-times before he's even born. It's the name that his parents choose for him.

We easily recognize the importance of a name in molding a person's experience when that name is ex-treme or ridiculous. For example, Johnny Cash sang a song about "A Boy Named Sue" several years ago. When he reached manhood, Sue searched the country for his long-lost father, in order to get even with him for his name. It seems that he had had to fight and experi-ence rejection at every turn as a result of his name.

But our names subtly mold our egos even when those names aren't extreme. One of my former teachers, John MacDavid, conducted a study that reveals the impor-tance of names. He found that children with names like David, Michael, and Patrick were rated as much more popular and likeable people than children with names like Sylvester, Percival, or Elmer.

Even common names can have a strong influence upon our likeability. Von Leirer,[1] a social psychologist, recently concluded that if Jimmy Carter had called him-self James, he might still be president.

Leirer drew his conclusions from a study comparing the three names: *James* (the formal name), *Jim* (the famil-iar name), and *Jimmy* (the adolescent one). He wrote a story about a person with one of those names. Different people were given the same story, but for some the person was named James, for some Jim, and for others Jimmy. They were then asked to rate the personality characteristics of people with these three names.

The study participants rated the person with the formal name *James* as less extroverted, more conscientious, more emotionally stable, and more cultivated than the ones with the familiar or adolescent names.

Clearly, the name you are called can affect people's first impressions. A middle-aged man who is called Johnny may be perceived differently from one who is called John. The way others perceive us, in turn, molds the way we perceive ourselves.

Some names are clearly masculine, and may encourage a stronger feeling of masculine security. Rock, Biff, and Chad suggest supermasculinity. Men with these names may grow into the name by cultivating their masculine characteristics. (It's also possible that they would feel more comfortable engaging in "feminine" behaviors. It's hard to snicker at a man baking bread if his name is Rocky.)

On the other hand, some names might lead a man to be somewhat defensive about his masculinity. "Bruce" has been associated, at least among comedians, with homosexuality. "Lynn" and "Pat" are unisex names—both men and women go by them. These names might create a few unpleasant experiences for men who have them.

Probably the first recorded example of a man who was extremely upset by his name occurs in the Old Testament. It concerns a man named Jabez. 1 Chronicles 4:9–10 tells his story:

Jabez came to more honour than his kinsmen. His mother had called him Jabez (Hurt), crying, "It hurt me to bear him." But

Jabez appealed to the God of Israel, "Oh that thou wouldest prosper me and enlarge my lot! Oh that thine hand might aid me! Oh that thou wouldest ward me from evil, that no hurt may befall me!" And God granted him what he asked (MOFFAT).

Sometime early in life Jabez must have realized his name meant "hurt." Perhaps his mother even reminded him of it occasionally. And since in biblical times names were often prophetic, Jabez probably put two and two together and figured that he might hurt someone else one day just as he had hurt his mother. He grew up expecting the worst from life, fearing every day that he would commit some evil, violent crime. So great was his insecurity that he was driven to his knees, pleading with God to overrule the curse of his name and to bless him.

The Parents' Marriage

Another important molder of the male ego, especially the part of it that women see, is the way a man's parents got along as husband and wife. Children observe the way their parents treat each other and react to each other. They learn about how men should relate to women, and vice versa, from those interactions.

One important lesson a man learns from those interactions is how to treat women. The way he sees his father treat his mother strongly influences the way a man will treat his own wife. If his father mistreats his mother, the son will probably learn to do the same. On the other hand, if he actively rebels against the father, he may go in the opposite direction; he may treat women with exceptional kindness to compensate for his father's rudeness. Other factors, such as personality style, birth order, and his own feelings about his father also play a role.

A young man I knew in college took the path of rebellion against his father. Craig was barely a teen-ager when his father left home, but Craig remembered enough about his father to know that he didn't want to be like him. His father had mistreated his mother, especially financially. He had given her little money to run the house while he spent lavishly on luxuries for himself. When he deserted the family, Craig's father sent little or no money back to them, so Craig's mom had to do housework for other people just to pay the bills.

When Craig married, he began right away to improve upon the example his father had set. He was very generous with his wife. If he had any money to spare he gave it to his wife to spend as she saw fit. In later years, when Craig had gained financial prosperity, he allowed his wife unlimited access to the checkbook. Craig's wife once told me that he, unlike his father, "would probably lay down his life" for her if necessary.

The quality of the parents' marriage is also an important influence on the quality a man will strive for in his own marriage. If the parents had a good marriage, the son will be more likely to want a good marriage himself; he will often be ready to make the necessary changes and put in the necessary amount of work to have a good marriage.

This was the case with Rick. He had grown up in a close-knit family where his mom and dad had shared everything, both the good and the bad. He had seen the laughter, the tears, the arguments, and the reconciliations. Married life meant intensity and intimacy for

Rick. He married Rachel, a young woman whose parents had a superficial relationship; they never fought, but they never really had a good time together either. They just lived together and tried to get along while keeping all their true feelings under wraps.

Rick found Rachel a warm and enthusiastic wife, but he noticed that she felt more comfortable keeping her distance from him. Whenever he would try to get her to open up emotionally, to express anger, for example, she would back away from him. Rick talked to Rachel about intimacy and how important it was to him. Still he made very little progress with her. But Rick did not give up. He spent ten years teaching his wife how to have a close emotional bond with him. He gave her books, he talked with her, he showed her by example what he was striving for. And very slowly, very gradually Rachel and Rick gained the intimacy that he had longed for. The vision of his parents' marriage kept him going until he achieved his goal.

One area that has particular relevance for most women is how communicative their husbands are. In part, men learn the skills of communication in marriage from observing their parents communicate. If the parents could communicate freely, the son will have at least the potential skill to communicate in his own marriage. But if they avoided communication, he may not even have the potential to do so himself. He may have to learn it strictly through trial and error.

I recently counseled a middle-aged married couple where the husband wouldn't communicate with his wife. He had grown up in a home where his parents hardly spoke to each other outside the sphere of formal requests ("Would you please pass the butter?"). Communication was a strange experience for him—one that he didn't handle very well. Though his marriage was in danger of breaking up because of his inability to express himself, he still found it extremely difficult to open up. When he did talk, he felt so uncomfortable that he quickly looked for ways to end the conversation. "I talk just for Myra's sake," he said. "I don't like it, but she needs it." He never acquired the desire to communicate, and so he talked only when she pushed hard for it.

Another area where the parents' marriage affects the son's ego is in the realm of conflict. Were the parents free to disagree with each other? Could they tolerate a difference of opinion? Could they listen to each other and accept the other person's point of view, even if they disagreed? Did they have good methods of resolving conflict without letting it get out of hand? Did they sweep conflict and disagreement under the rug?

It's important for married couples to get along. But it's also important for them to accept their disagreements and demonstrate ways to resolve those areas of conflict. If a couple won't allow any conflict to surface, then later in life their son may see any disagreement on his wife's part as a threat to his status and ego. If a couple disagree too much and too often, especially about how to discipline their son, he may see other people's opinions as too unreliable. But if they can handle their areas of conflict well, their child will learn not to be threatened by differences of opinion. When he marries he will be able to tolerate areas where he and his wife are not in agreement.

The Father's Influence

The type and quality of relationship a boy has with his father is one of the most crucial factors in his ego and personality development. The way his father treats him, how much time the two spend together, and how strong an influence the father had upon him go a long way toward influencing the way a man presents himself to the world and the way the world responds to him in turn.

The mother's influence is crucial, too, especially in the early years. But mothers can more often be counted on to develop a close relationship with their children. Fathers, on the other hand, show a wide range of commitments. Many are absent altogether; some are there but are ineffective; a few (far too few) are good fathers to their children.

For years, our society fostered the idea that all children needed for their emotional health was adequate mothering. The father simply brought home the bacon. But behavioral scientists have learned a lot since then. We now know that fathers are vitally important, too, in a different way from mothers.

Psychologist Lois Hoffman reviewed the research on the effects of fathering and mothering several years ago. She concluded that each makes a unique contribution to the child's development: "From our data, it would appear that a mother's love and attention make a boy feel warm and cozy, but a father's equip him to face the world."[2] Probably the best collection of research on fathering is in Michael Lamb's *The Role of the Father in Child Development*.[3] When the children of absent, ineffective, and effective fathers are compared, the children of the effective fathers consistently turn out to have the following advantages:

Higher self-esteem
Higher self-confidence

More popular
More often chosen as leaders
More emotionally stable, less anxious
Better students, with higher grades
Better workers, more industrious
Better behaved, less often delinquents or criminals
Better husbands and fathers themselves

Other differences also showed up, but these most directly involve the ego. Surprisingly, one conclusion the research offers is that men who had a good relationship with their own fathers seem better able to get along with women. Perhaps they are more secure and better able to handle the give and take of an intimate relationship.

One qualification to these findings is that if the child is close to his father, but he views his mother as undesirable, he may grow up despising all that is feminine. I once counseled a middle-aged man who had a very close, warm relationship with his father but despised his mother, who was an alcoholic. He grew up with a secure sense of masculinity and a disgust with everything feminine. He went through three marriages marred by conflict and verbal warfare.

The Impact of Puberty

Puberty is a big event for a male. He ceases being a boy and becomes instead a young man. His sexuality emerges as his body changes. His physique begins to resemble that of a man, instead of a child, as his musculature develops. As a result of these changes, he becomes more attractive to women and more physically competitive with men.

All this doesn't happen overnight, of course. It goes on for several years. But it is a rather dramatic process. Teachers who don't see their adolescent students during the entire summer often remark about the changes that took place between spring and fall: "I can't believe how much you've grown!"

These changes are not lost on the adolescent. How much he changes with puberty and the timing of the changes have a profound impact upon a young man.

One of the most interesting research studies on adolescence investigated the impact of early and late puberty upon young men's development.[4] The study divided a sample of adolescent males into two groups: early maturers (those who reached puberty around age twelve) and late maturers (those who reached puberty around age fourteen or fifteen). The researchers followed these two groups of men into their early forties to see if early or late puberty had a lasting effect. It did.

From the very beginning, all sorts of differences showed up between the two groups. The researchers asked the teachers and classmates of these students to describe them. Consistently the early maturers were described as more attractive, more mature, more popular, and more socially skilled than the late maturers, who were more often rejected by peers and teachers alike. (Interestingly, the late maturers became the "class clowns" as a way of getting attention.)

The researchers then gave personality questionnaires to the two groups to find out how they saw themselves. Again the late maturers were found wanting. They had poorer self-images, less self-confidence, and felt less attractive than the early maturers. (Again, interestingly, they tended to blame their parents for the problems associated with a late puberty.)

You'd hope that by the early thirties these differences would have ironed themselves out. But not so. When the researchers again studied these young men at the beginning of middle age, the early maturers were better off. They were more socially active, more successful at work, and more involved in their communities. The late maturers had one advantage, though. They had happier, more stable marriages.

By the mid-forties, however, the advantages of being an early maturer were beginning to fade. The late maturers had just about caught up with their early-maturing peers in occupational success, and they still had more stable marriages.

So late maturity creates at least the potential for a variety of ego problems. Men who reach puberty late are more insecure and less socially skilled. But the curse comes with a blessing. They also seem to make more faithful husbands. Perhaps male ego problems are not all bad.

Marriage and Intimacy

After puberty, the next major ego stage for a man is adjusting to the process of developing an intimate relationship with a woman. In order to be successful, he must meet and master two tasks: (1) He must learn to appreciate the differences between himself and his wife, and (2) he must learn the skills of intimacy.

Learning to appreciate a woman is part of the process of learning to appreciate sexual differences. When men and women can really appreciate what their mates bring to the relationship, many of the ego and adjustment problems associated with heterosexual relationships will disappear.

In fact, this is so important to marriage that it has been successfully used to treat homosexuality. Recently a philosophy entitled Aesthetic Realism, based upon the teachings of the poet Eli Siegel, has gained prominence. Siegel made the following observations, which are central tenets of the philosophy:

1. All homosexuality arises from contempt for the world, and contempt for what is different.
2. Because men and women are biologically and emotionally different, these dislikes change into contempt for the opposite sex.
3. The way to like the world, and the things in it, is to see "the aesthetic ones of opposites."[5]

The program involves such mental exercises as visualizing a girl dancing, focusing on her grace and the softness of her flesh, while thinking about the strength required for her to dance and the hardness of her bones. The lesson is that beauty lies in the contrast. That is an important lesson for homosexuals, who are repulsed by the differences between men and women.

David Twomley, a researcher for WABC-TV in New York and a former homosexual who was actively involved in the gay rights movement, went through the Aesthetic Realism program and as a result abandoned homosexuality for "the completeness that a woman brings to a man's life." David is now married, and on his first wedding anniversary reported that "I feel like singing. . . . I feel like telling everyone in the country 'I love my wife.'"

A similar process goes on among men with successful marriages. In fact, this appreciation of women and of the differences between the two sexes is a vital contributor toward controlling many of the male ego problems that women dislike.

A second task that a man faces upon marrying is to move toward an intimate relationship with his spouse. Intimacy is hard for some people to deal with. It brings with it a kind of dependence that some find frightening. And it makes demands on the two spouses that all too many lack the resources to handle.

This was the problem that Charles and Patsy faced when they came to my office. Charles and Patsy came from two very different backgrounds. Patsy had six brothers and sisters and grew up in a very close-knit family. Charles, on the other hand, was an only child whose father spent most of his time on the road as a truckdriver. So Charles and Patsy entered marriage with two completely different ideas about intimacy.

Patsy needed a lot of communication, a lot of sharing; but Charles felt more comfortable alone. He worked all day and took courses in the evening so he rarely had the time or energy to become really close to his wife. When he finished school, he had more time on his hands; but he soon got heavily involved in church activities.

When Charles got a job promotion and he and Patsy moved to a new state, Charles couldn't find a church he wanted to attend regularly. "Now," thought Patsy, "now finally we'll be able to spend some time together and develop a really deep relationship." But Charles began watching TV almost obsessively. He turned it on the minute he came home from work in the evening and watched it until after Patsy went to sleep. He watched TV all weekend, too. Patsy finally resigned herself to an incomplete marriage, even though she still longed for a deep emotional sharing with Charles. She realized that he feared intimacy so much that he would always run away from it, hiding himself in some activity.

Intimacy doesn't simply mean sharing the good times—although that's part of it. Intimacy has been defined as the ability to share hurt, meaning that couples who are truly intimate will sometimes hurt each other. But they will then share that hurt. They won't require the other person to bear it alone.

Intimacy seems to be more difficult for men than for women. But the advantages are considerable: greater physical health results from the security of intimacy, and intimate couples are happier in their marriages. But intimacy requires giving up a lopsided amount of power and making yourself vulnerable. That is the price of intimacy. The rewards are tremendous. But there are costs as well.

Birth of the First Child

The birth of a man's first child often brings about ego changes so subtle that only the most alert wife will know what's going on.

Let's say that a man and woman have been successful in setting up a reasonably intimate and rewarding relationship in the first few months or years of marriage. Then along comes their first child. All of a sudden, the pattern they've worked so hard to establish becomes hard to maintain.

The first casualty is the husband. Very quickly he faces a dramatic reduction in the amount of attention and care he receives from his wife. Her attention goes elsewhere. It has to. And he realizes that. But still . . . something feels wrong.

At that point he probably turns a little bit more toward work, toward the TV, toward his buddies after work, or toward another woman if he's not careful.

Then his wife starts to feel the pinch of child-rearing. She wants increased support from him at a time when he's experiencing a decrease in support from her. She wants him to take over more with the child; but he is starting to resent his new rival, and finds it difficult to take over enthusiastically a job she's more competent at and more comfortable with.

If the two aren't careful, they can find themselves growing increasingly distant. At that point the husband needs to call up the philosophy of masculinity that says fathering is a noble task for men. This may be difficult, because for the first few months it may seem as though the child does not really need him that much. But he can and should play a vital role in his child's development right from the start.

The mother also needs to be aware of what's going on with her husband. It's easy for him to feel shut out of the twosome that his wife and child have become. She needs to take pains to include him and to show that her commitment to him is still alive by setting up time to be with him. Wrapped up as she is in the job of motherhood, it's easy for her to lose interest in his world at a time when he probably needs an even greater demonstration of interest.

The Mid-Life Crisis

The next big ego event that a man faces is the mid-life crisis. It's called a crisis because how he resolves it can determine his future happiness. If he successfully passes through it, he will be stronger and happier in the future. If he fails or miffs some of the tasks the crisis requires, he may make a shambles of his life and have recurring ego problems.

In our culture, the mid-life crisis is probably inevitable to one degree or another for most men. We worship youth and beauty. And we're not too kind to our elderly. This is not the case in many other cultures. Often the elderly are venerated for their wisdom and experience. In those cultures men don't have mid-life crises.

The man going through a mid-life crisis in our culture experiences his aging as a loss. And since loss commonly leads to depression, one of his most compelling characteristics is frequent mood swings. He undergoes periods where his energy level drops and his interest in life plummets. His self-esteem is low, and the things that used to make him feel worthwhile, such as his achievements, no longer seem important to him.

Generally the wives of men in mid-life crises report that their husbands demonstrate an acute change in behavior. "This usually loving, positive man suddenly became negative, hostile, and moody," they report.

Instead of sharing his feelings with others, the man in mid-life crisis is compelled to keep distant and uncommunicative. He can't, or won't, talk about it. This drives his wife crazy; she is having a crisis from his crisis and wants some answers.

But he can't talk to her about his feelings because his feelings tell him that his wife and the marriage are to blame for his crisis. He feels trapped, and he blames everything he once loved—wife, marriage, children, job—for his emotional state. As a result, he feels sorry for himself.

On the whole, the mid-life crisis sounds like adolescence, and that's what it is—a second adolescence, a transitional state where he's neither an elderly nor a young man. He will soon enter an entirely different stage in his life—one that will see the entire culture treating him differently.

The mid-life crisis can occur at anytime between the ages of thirty and sixty, but usually it unfolds in the mid-to-late forties. That's the transitional period between the productive years and the retirement years.

I've seen mid-life crises fairly often among men in their mid-thirties. In every case, these men didn't have a typical adolescence. Either they married early and didn't have a chance to date very many women, or their parents were excessively strict and legalistic, completely squelching any moves the young man made toward independence. The inability to have a successful first adolescence hastened the coming of the second adolescence.

This is what happened to David, a man I'm counseling. He grew up in an authoritarian family with a strict religious background. His parents kept a tight rein on him all during his teen-age years. The first time David really tasted freedom was when he went away to college, but right away he met a girl he really liked and began dating her exclusively. They married while still in college, mainly because David liked the security that marriage offered. He lacked the self-confidence to try his luck with other girls, so he thought it made good sense to marry his sweetheart and avoid the possible pain and rejection that might occur if he went out with other girls.

But once David graduated from college and got established in a successful career, his confidence shot up. He felt good about himself and about his ability to attract women. He began to wish that he'd dated more in college, that he'd gotten to know many women instead of just one. He thought more and more about what he had missed. Soon he became sexually involved with one of his colleagues at work, then later with one of his wife's friends. He also became depressed over the meaninglessness of life. David sailed smoothly through his teen-age years only to find life crashing down around him in his mid-thirties.

Families in which the father is having a mid-life crisis can be very frustrating to treat from a counseling standpoint. Little can be done to shorten the stage. Since the wives are justifiably distraught, marital counseling can alleviate a few of the problems. But usually all a counselor can do is give her emotional support to help her through it.

The main key to a successful mid-life crisis is the man. Can he go through it without making major changes in his life when he feels low? In general, major life decisions should not be made when you're depressed. So the major task the man at mid-life faces is to hang in there until he can sort out all the various forces that are impinging on him and forge out a new identity for himself. If he lets the extramarital affair that is so common during the crisis pull him out of his marriage, or if he turns away from his work or his family, he may seriously damage his chances for a happy future.

So the major message for men during this stage is "hang on." Don't let your emotional state cause you to reject the things you truly love and value. That love will reawaken when the crisis is resolved. The worst thing would be to come out of the crisis to find the things you truly love gone.

Retirement

Retirement is the last ego stage that most men face. It is a critical time, requiring adjustment and reordering of priorities.

To some men, retirement is almost a completely positive experience. They look forward to doing the things they want to do, instead of having to follow the dictates of a structured job. They become more relaxed and human, showing a side of themselves no one saw before.

This was John's experience with retirement. His job had kept him under a lot of pressure. He always had to prove himself to his fellow workers; and when he came home from work, he carried the stress and tension with him. But when he retired, all that changed. He became a different person. Friends and family members noticed right away that he was more relaxed and sociable. His children, who had always been a little hesitant to interact with him, suddenly found him warm and anxious to talk. He worked on hobbies that he hadn't had time to pursue before. He dabbled in real estate, built a new room on his home, and rebuilt two or three antique cars. His life became full and rewarding.

But for many men, especially those who have come to define their masculinity by their achievements, retirement is a mixed blessing. In order to feel good about it, they must learn to enjoy themselves without feeling guilty that they're not producing. They must learn to listen to a new voice, one that's stronger than the voice that says, "You're not worthwhile as a man unless you have a job and are achieving." For many men, especially those who have been listening to that voice alone over the years and who thus haven't cultivated other standards of masculinity such as fathering and family, the old voice may be too loud to drown out. Many stories have been told of men who die six months after they retire.

Some men also interpret retirement as a loss rather than as a gain—a loss of potency, status, and structure. Those men take retirement hard. For them, the loss goes deeper than just an external standard of masculine worth; they see it as a loss of their very manhood. Often sexual impotence results as they feel unable to perform even in the bedroom.

This is an unfortunate overgeneralization. Those men need to see retirement as a gain, rather than as a loss, and as a sign of their potency rather than their impotence. Retirement says, first of all, that you're fortunate to have lived long enough to retire. Many men don't. But above that, it says that you've been an effective worker for years and years. You did your job well and your retirement is an acknowledgement of your effectiveness. No one loses their potency the minute they retire, unless they tell themselves over and over again that they will.

Another problem that retirement creates for many men is, "What do I do with my time?" Even very creative and resourceful men may flounder about for several months as they attempt to refine the ability to locate activities they enjoy.

Newly retired men often begin to place an increasing number of demands on their wives—demands for attention, time, and activities to do together. This was the very behavior that Walt's wife described to me when they came in for counseling. Walt had a heart attack and was forced to retire early from a high-level position in management. Once he recovered physically, he felt lost without a job to go to each day. He'd never had so much free time on his hands and didn't know what to do with himself all day long. So he looked to his wife, Carol, to structure his time for him and to keep him entertained. At the same time, he developed the habit of watching Carol's every move and giving her a running commentary of what he thought about her lifestyle. If this wasn't hard enough for Carol to take, soon after Walt's retirement their daughter had a new baby and she had to go help her. Walt, of course, went along, too. Now Carol had to care for her daughter, her grandchild, *and* her husband. Just about the time Carol would start dinner or go to change the baby, Walt would want her to sit and talk with him. If she started to fold diapers or take the baby out in the stroller, Walt would ask her to watch TV with him. The situation got so bad that this happily-married, stable couple had to seek counseling for the first time in their lives.

Many wives, like Carol, feel swamped with their husbands' demands. And a woman's stress can be worsened if her husband also goes into a depression or begins to blame her for his situation.

But if the two of them are willing to talk about the changes that retirement has brought about in his lifestyle, and the deeper meanings that retirement has for his conceptions of his own masculinity, they can usually be successful in helping him past this final ego stage. His ego was initially formed in the family; and fittingly it's the family that helps him battle with this final ego stage.

TWELVE

Work and Love

The two areas where men live most of their psychological lives are work and love. And these two arenas are so closely associated that what happens in one often affects the other.

A man who feels successful in love should find his attitude toward work improving. If love from others is the basis for self-love, as some have asserted, then the man who feels love should have a confidence that the unloved man doesn't experience.

But the opposite relationship seems to be even more important: the man who feels successful in work will find it much easier to enter the world of love successfully than the unsuccessful man. Work has become the proving ground for the male ego. It is the one role society must insure for men if they are to feel good about themselves as men.

Men not only rely upon society for their work roles, but they also rely upon a woman's need for and assessment of that role. "What difference does my life make?" men ask. And the answer they receive depends *in large part upon the difference their role makes in the lives of their women*. If a man's role is important to his woman (and to a lesser extent, to his children), he will feel more secure. This is why the provider role is so important to the male

[242]

ego. It is the tangible, meaningful contribution to women and to the family that he desperately needs to make.

Joe grew up in the ghetto. The oldest of five children, he had seen his father desert the family, leaving his mother to struggle to make some kind of decent life for the children. Joe decided very early that he would never follow in his father's footsteps; he hated what his father's absence had done to his mother and all the children, and he vowed that he would someday take care of his own family so well that it would make up for his father's desertion.

Joe married Lee Ann the week they both graduated from high school. Within a few years they had a nice apartment and a baby on the way. Everything seemed to be going exactly according to Joe's timetable. Then he got laid off at work. At first he thought it was a temporary slow-down at the plant, but soon Joe realized that he had better look for work somewhere else. Every day he pored over the want ads, called potential employers, and went on job interviews. But there were just too few jobs to go around, and Joe was forced to go on unemployment insurance. Lee Ann continued to work right up until the baby came and then went back to work six weeks later. Joe kept the baby, but every day was like a nightmare for him.

He felt useless, helpless, depressed, and frustrated all at once. The baby was fretful, wanting only her mother. And to make matters worse, Lee Ann began complaining about how much work she had to do. She began nagging Joe about helping her with the cooking, washing, ironing, and house-cleaning. This was more than Joe could take; he was a husband, not a wife. One day he left his daughter with a neighbor and just disappeared.

Joe had a strong desire to provide for his family. When he could no longer fill that role, when it seemed that his wife could fill every important role in the family better than he could, Joe felt estranged from the home, no longer a real part of the family, and so he left.

It would be tempting to conclude that this emphasis upon work is some personal hangup that men have. But studies indicate that women need their men to succeed no less than the men need it.

Earning power is one area where the male ego shows a painful hypersensitivity. If men don't earn at least as much as their wives, bad things happen in the marriage to both partners.

These surprising observations were reported recently by Dr. Carin Rubenstein, a social psychologist and associate editor of *Psychology Today*.[1] Dr. Rubenstein reviewed numerous studies that investigated homes in which wives earned more money than their husbands and found that "this situation can be disastrous for marriages, and especially debilitating for men." For example, not only did many of these men feel that their wives loved them less than they loved their wives, but their sex lives were also in jeopardy. About 17 percent of the men questioned reported that they had not had sexual relations at all for several months before answering the survey. Not surprisingly, those men had low self-esteem and were dissatisfied with marriage, family, and friends alike.

As unfortunate as these problems are, Dr. Rubenstein reported yet another research finding that underscores even more dramatically the devastating effects when a man loses the role of major provider. Not only does the loss of that role produce emotional and psychological damage, but it actually takes a heavy physical toll as well. Specifically, Dr. Rubenstein found that husbands who earn less than their wives *die prematurely from heart disease eleven times more often than husbands who outearn their wives.*

Men aren't the only losers when wives have greater earning capacities. Dr. Rubenstein found that many of these high-income wives didn't love their husbands (three times higher than low-income wives), had poor sexual adjustment, and were obsessed with money, having frequent arguments with their husbands over household finances. Often their problems outweighed the joys of marriage, and divorce seemed the only way out.

Because success at work is so crucial to the male ego, it is difficult for many men to find that delicate balance between involvement in work and involvement in love. Oftentimes they resolve the dilemma by swinging wildly back and forth between the two extremes.

Consider the case of Mike and Cindy. They had a happy, stable family. Mike was the manager for a building supply company and Cindy stayed home to care for their two boys. There was never an abundance of money, but they had plenty to meet their needs. Everything was going along well until Mike lost his job and had to take a very undemanding position as a guard at a warehousing company. Suddenly Mike was isolated from people all day, and he began to lean heavily on Cindy for emotional support. He would call her four or five times a day to see if she had any news to relate—which she never did. He would come home for lunch every day, and in the evenings he craved Cindy's un-divided attention. Cindy soon realized that Mike was totally bored with his job, and that at the same time he was starved for human interaction. She encouraged him to look for work elsewhere, which he gladly did.

But as the weeks turned into months and no new job turned up, Mike became depressed and hostile. He avoided his friends and relatives, preferring the quiet isolation of his home. When he did go out, people frequently commented that Mike was a changed man. Cindy knew they were right. Mike had changed, and now she felt trapped and frustrated. She kept thinking, "Things couldn't possibly be worse."

Finally Mike found a position in a government supply agency. He was back in a job in which he felt comfortable, and he quickly made friends with his new associates. Both he and Cindy felt their problems were over. Mike, in fact, was so anxious to do well in his job that he began working overtime several nights a week. He joined the office bowling team and even went out to eat with his fellow employees. At first Cindy felt lonely. Mike was never home anymore. Then her loneliness turned to frustration and anger. Often Mike left for work before she awoke in the morning and returned home after she was asleep at night. When he was home, he was so tired he fell asleep right in the middle of a conversation. Cindy's social life was nonexistent. She couldn't invite friends to her home because Mike was either not there or else was sound asleep.

Cindy, in a few short months, had experienced two extremes—too much time with Mike and then no time with him at all. At one end of the spectrum Mike had placed nearly all his ego needs on their relationship; he had depended on Cindy for everything. Later, at the other extreme, he had become so totally involved with work that he had no relationship with Cindy whatsoever.

It is not because they are very similar that work and love have such an effect on each other. They are, in fact, quite opposite. Work requires a different set of attributes and behaviors from love. Work is structured and very product-oriented; love is spontaneous and relationship-oriented. Work involves getting ahead and advancing one's self; love involves submerging one's self.

It's very hard for many men to integrate these two opposites. They find it difficult to leave the world of goals and productivity to enter the world of relationships. Oftentimes men bring their work attitudes home. "I've produced a fine son," a man will say, with the same orientation he would have toward a widget. Or he'll be *with* the family but not involved *in* the family, preferring instead his magazine or the TV. Or he'll see his home as a comfortable rest break between his excursions to the office or factory instead of a place where true living really takes place.

In part this is because men find work more compatible with their egos than love. The distance, productivity, and abstractness of work come more easily to men than the less-structured, other-orientation of love and family.

Love and family life are strange new experiences for men, requiring new skills that are difficult for them to attain. They have to work at them. And they're already working at . . . work.

It's hard for men to drop an attitude that they have to adopt for at least eight hours a day and pick up one that didn't come easily to begin with. But this is a necessary task for the man with a secure and buoyant ego. Both arenas are important in order to be fully alive. For many men, it's the area of love that suffers.

Dr. Jay Rohrlich, a psychiatrist, wrote an interesting book entitled *Work and Love: The Crucial Balance.*[2] In it, he observes that men so often allow work to interfere with love that they become addicted to work. Work becomes their sole source of self-esteem and satisfaction in life. He mentions several characteristics of work addicts. Those characteristics sound like masculine orientation carried to the extreme. The work addict, according to Dr. Rohrlich, will usually show several of the following characteristics:

1. The work addict is fiercely skill-oriented. Every situation involves skills and goals. He either avoids more intimate relationships or redefines them as situations that require "intimacy skills" or "relationship skills."

These men don't feel comfortable in the world of emotion and spontaneity. They are locked into the attitude that everything is a performance requiring certain skills to be successful. That approach to life, so successful in the world of work, doesn't carry over well into the world of social relationships and family.

2. The work addict is also locked into a fiercely analytical attitude. Everything is broken down into categories and examined, weighed, and evaluated. Even love must be defined before it can be experienced.

3. A work addict lives by the aggressive instinct. He must constantly manipulate and control his environment in order to feel comfortable. He can't enjoy a movie, for example, without thinking how he might have done it differently.

4. The work addict can't live in the present unless it involves creating a product. He has to be planning, organizing, and inventing for the future.

5. Efficiency is the work addict's most cherished goal. Everything must give way or become efficient. Time is not to be wasted. Every minute must be tied to some purpose or productive activity.

As Dr. Rohrlich points out, this attitude stands in contrast to the one that upholds love and human relationships. Both love and work are important, and optimally each man will strive to find a balance between the two in his own life.

That balance is becoming increasingly harder to achieve in modern societies. The breakdown of the family has made human relationships, for many people, untrustworthy. So they must concentrate on work. Interestingly, high unemployment rates don't seem to create the opposite philosophy. No one has yet written a book whose message is, "Jobs can't be trusted. Throw yourself into human relationships." Maybe the reason is that most people who write books are themselves extremely product-oriented.

But if a man is to live life to the fullest (and if a woman is to enjoy her man fully) he must learn to define himself—his masculine self-worth—in terms of the world of love as well as the world of work. Men who adopt loving relationships as part of their definition of self will have greater resources with which to ride out the bumps and bruises of life than men who throw their entire self-worth into work.

One of the most discouraging trends I've observed in today's society is one that encourages men to place even less of their egos into their love relationships than they already do. For example, the press has recently become enamored with a growing social trend—women who choose to become single mothers. These women are generally successful professionals who want children, but not the demands of living with a husband. They either don't tell the father they're pregnant or they are artificially inseminated. Their actions say they consider fathers unimportant. So a generation of children will grow up without attachment to a male parent, and men will have the idea that they are not really needed or wanted in the home. Thus, fathering becomes less and less a part of their egos.

Similarly, some women are driving men further away from letting their egos become involved in loving relationships by asserting that men are not as important to women as, say, jobs.

That's just the sort of message that further encourages men not to see loving relationships as an important source of masculine self-worth. It further upholds the world of work as superior to and more important than the world of love. And it tells men not to put too much of themselves into loving relationships.

These trends are ultimately destructive. In a world where love and human relationships are rapidly fragmenting, the last thing we need to hear is that they weren't very important in the first place.

The fact is that men are vitally important in their homes and to their women. Likewise, men hold a crucial role in the world of work. Only by emphasizing both arenas can men have truly secure egos.

That balance between the two arenas would go a long

way toward building strong male egos. But something is still missing. What's needed is a glue to hold it all together, an overarching purpose to give meaning to both our love and our work, as well as to our lives. It is to that topic that we turn in the last chapter.

THIRTEEN

The Higher Purpose

Our grandparents and their ancestors had an advantage that increasingly we are denying ourselves. They had a higher purpose that gave meaning to their lives and that gave their activities and experiences a sense of meaning beyond their own immediate merits.

For one thing, they had a work ethic that made their efforts a way of glorifying God. They worked hard for the same reasons we work hard: to live comfortably, have things, succeed, and satisfy ego needs. But they also worked hard because they felt that their work was a way of worshiping God. As a result, they probably worked more efficiently and felt better about what they were doing than most of us do today.

They also had the conviction that their relationships were sacred, and that what they did within those relationships reflected upon God Himself. This is no doubt one reason why divorces were so rare in their time.

In other words, everything they did was uplifted by the sense of a higher purpose. And thus they found greater meaning in what they did because of that purpose. And they found comfort in the knowledge that just as they acted to glorify God, so God also intervened in their lives.

"We know that all things work together for good to

those who love God, to those who are the called according to His purpose" (Rom. 8:28). That verse serves not only as a comfort to those who believe it, but it also puts a check on the ego problems that are likely to afflict many men in today's world. It is difficult for men who believe that statement to demonstrate outrageous reactions to either success or setback for very long.

I remember living for several years in a situation that I thought intolerable. And I prayed for deliverance. Nothing happened. For three years nothing happened. Then, when I thought there was no hope, it all changed so suddenly I could scarcely follow everything that went on. I believe the changes were wrought by the hand of God. I believe He had a plan for my life. And when the time was right, He changed things for the better.

The belief that God has a personalized, individualized plan for our lives can go a long way toward reducing, or eliminating, the fears and insecurities that afflict men. God created us male and female. And He knows that we need certain things specific to our sex. Just as He took care of Sarah by giving her a child, so He can also take care of men by giving them jobs to fulfill their role as provider.

But our relationship with God is also important in helping us deal with the opposite types of ego problems. Arrogance, egotism, and grandiosity are no less serious ego problems than insecurity or self-doubt. "For I say, through the grace given unto me, to every man that is among you, not to think of himself more highly than he ought to think; but to think soberly, according as God hath dealt to every man the measure of faith" (Rom. 12:3 KJV).

The Christian message is one of self-sacrificing love

and a willingness to put self behind higher principles. Christ had it all—the power, the adoration, and the wealth. And yet He put it aside. He was not willing to allow self to get out of control. And He bids us follow Him.

He was able to make His sacrifice for mankind because His life was governed by higher principles. We have Him as a model. If we look to Him, our egos won't get too far out of proportion.

Notes

Chapter 3
1. Carol Tavris and Carole Offir, *The Longest War* (New York: Harcourt, Brace, Jovanovich, 1977).
2. Barbara Forisha, *Sex Roles and Personal Awareness* (New Jersey: Scott, Foresman, and Company, 1978).
3. Anne Erhardt and Susan Baker, "Fetal Androgens, Human Central Nervous System Differentiation, and Behavior Sex Differences," *Sex Differences in Behavior*, R. C. Friedman et.al., eds. (New York: Wiley, 1974).
4. Margaret Mead, *Male and Female* (New York: Morrow, 1949).
5. George Gilder, *Sexual Suicide* (New York: Quadrangle, 1973).
6. Ibid.

Chapter 4
1. Hans Eysenck, *Personality Structure and Measurement* (London: Routledge and Kegan Paul, 1969).

Chapter 6
1. "Infertility: New Cures Bring New Hope," *Newsweek* (December 6, 1982).

Chapter 7
1. Carol Gilligan, *In a Different Voice* (Massachusetts: Harvard University Press, 1982).
2. Elizabeth Mehren, "A Case of Attempted Rape," *Newsweek* (March 14, 1983).

Chapter 9
1. Oscar Lewis, *La Vida: A Puerto-Rican Family in San Juan and New York* (New York: Irvington House, 1966).

2. Steven Goldberg, *The Inevitability of Patriarchy* (New York: Morrow, 1973).

3. Sandra Bem, "The Measurement of Psychological Androgyny," *Journal of Clinical and Counseling Psychology* 2 (1974), 153–62.

Chapter 10

1. Albert Ellis, *Reason and Emotion in Psychotherapy* (New York: Lyle Stuart, 1962).

2. Ed Hayes, "Artist-author laughs off rejection slips," *Orlando Sentinel* (April 24, 1982).

3. Harvey Brenner, "Out of Work, Out of Hope," *Orlando Sentinel* (April 3, 1983).

4. Robert Miller, "The Park Ridge, New Jersey, Experiment," *Guideposts* (November, 1982).

Chapter 11

1. "Call Me James!" *Psychology Today* (May, 1983).

2. L. W. Hoffman, "The Father's Role in the Family and the Child's Peer Group Adjustment," *Merrill Palmer Quarterly,* vol. 7 (1961).

3. Michael Lamb, *The Role of the Father in Child Development* (New York: John Wiley and Sons, 1976).

4. M. C. Jones and N. Bayley, "Physical Maturing among Boys as Related to Behavior," *Journal of Educational Psychology* 41 (1950), 129–148.

5. Jeffrey Zaslow, "Philosophy Shows Gay Men How to Appreciate Women," *Orlando Sentinel* (March 17,1983).

Chapter 12

1. Carin Rubenstein, "Real Men Don't Earn Less Than Their Wives," *Psychology Today* (November, 1982).

2. Jay Rohrlich, *Work and Love: The Crucial Balance* (New York: Harmony Books, 1980).